Backroad Bicycling in the Blue Ridge and Smoky Mountains

Steven Miller enjoying the Mouse Branch Loop at Tsali

Backroad Bicycling in the Blue Ridge and Smoky Mountains

HIRAM ROGERS

27 Rides for Touring
and Mountain Bikes
from North Georgia to
Southwest Virginia

Backcountry Guides
Woodstock, Vermont

AN INVITATION TO THE READER Although it is unlikely that the roads you cycle on these tours will change much with time, some road signs, landmarks, and other items may. If you find that such changes have occurred on these routes, please let the author and publisher know, so that corrections may be made in future editions. Other comments and suggestions are also welcome. Address all correspondence to: Editor, Backroad Bycycling Series, Backcountry Guides, P.O. Box 748, Woodstock, VT 05091.

ISBN 0-88150-576-5
ISSN 1547-3252

Cover and interior design by Bodenweber Design
Composition by PerfecType, Nashville, TN
Cover photograph © Dennis Coello
Interior photographs by the author, except as noted.

Published by Backcountry Guides, a division of The Countryman Press, P.O. Box 748, Woodstock, Vermont 05091

Distributed by W.W. Norton & Company, Inc., 500 Fifth Avenue, New York, NY 10110

Printed in the United States of America

10 9 8 7 6 5 4 3 2 1

I'm grateful for the support of my wife, Jean, who has helped with this project from start to finish. I couldn't imagine a better companion at home or on the trail. Jean reviewed much of the manuscript and rode many of the rides, including a few on days more suited for ark building than bike riding. Here's to many more adventures ahead of us.

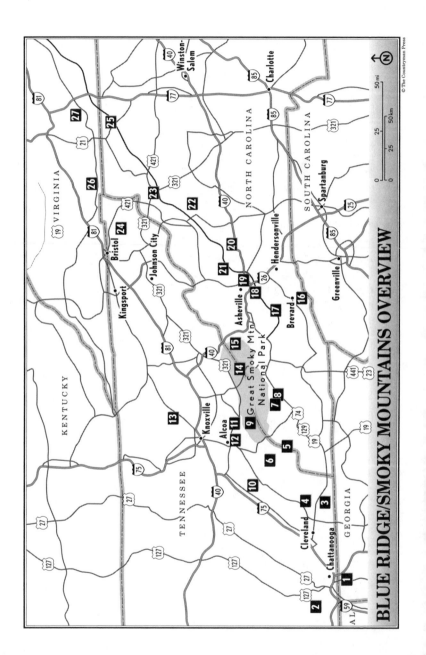

BLUE RIDGE/SMOKY MOUNTAINS OVERVIEW

© The Countryman Press

CONTENTS

ACKNOWLEDGMENTS Steven Miller provided welcome accommodations in Asheville, joined me on many rides both on and off the roads, proofed a number of chapters, and suggested the routes in the Asheville area. His patience during lengthy note taking and frequent photography stops is appreciated.

The following people were kind enough to review drafts of ride descriptions in their areas and provide many helpful comments: Nancy Gray, Great Smoky Mountains National Park; Pat Lockamy, Blue Ridge Parkway; and Sam Weddle, Chickamauga and Chattanooga National Military Park.

Many others were kind enough to answer my stream of questions, steer me away from problem areas, and guide me onto the region's best trails. A special thanks to: Diane Bolt, Pisgah Ranger District; Laney Cutshaw, Cheoah Ranger District; Frank Findley, Cheoah Ranger District; Steve Goldman, Ocoee Ranger District; Sherri Hicks, Ocoee Whitewater Center; Jim Lane, Prentice Cooper State Forest and Wildlife Management Area; Frank Lewis, Cherokee National Forest; and Mary Noel, National Forests in North Carolina.

BACKROAD BICYCLE TOURS AT A GLANCE

	TOUR	SURFACE	DISTANCE	SHO
1.	Chickamauga Battlefield	Paved	10.7	7.0
2.	Prentice Cooper	Dirt	15.2	10.2
3.	Ocoee	Trail	8.3	6.0
4.	Chilhowee	Trail	11.9	3.6
5.	Cherohala Skyway	Paved	15.3	9.7
6.	Jake Best–Doublecamp	Dirt	19.0	3.4
7.	Tsali Left Loop	Trail	12.0	7.7
8.	Tsali Mouse Branch Loop	Trail	10.2	7.3
9.	Cades Cove	Paved	10.7	3.7
10.	Foothills Parkway	Paved	17.7	9.6
11.	Little River	Paved	17.8	8.9
12.	Maryville-Alcoa Greenway	Paved	17.1	5.4
13.	House Mountain	Paved	27.9	14.4
14.	Balsam Mountain–Cherokee	Mixed	48.3	8.0
15.	Cataloochee	Mixed	12.7	5.8
16.	Brevard to Rosman	Paved	29.1	7.6

EXTRA	TYPE	BIKE	HIGHLIGHTS
18.0	Loop	R	Battlefield monuments
27.2	Loop	M	Tennessee River overlooks
17.9	Loop	M	New trails above Ocoee River
16.1	Loop	M	Benton Falls and Clemmer Trail
29.0	1-Way	R	Mountain views and Hooper Bald
30.4	Loop	M	Citico and Doublecamp Creeks
18.2	Loop	M	Singletrack on Fontana Lake
16.3	Loop	M	Lake views and singletrack
31.3	Loop	R	Mountain homesites
35.4	1-Way	R	Look Rock Tower
27.3	Rt	R	Rural roads on the Little River
34.2	Rt	R	Springbrook and Greenbelt Parks
49.1	Loop	R	Rural farms and mountain views
53.1	Loop	M	Views of forests and rivers
40.7	Loop	M	Elk herd and historic buildings
41.0	Loop	R	East Fork and French Broad Rivers

	TOUR	SURFACE	DISTANCE	SHC
17.	Pisgah to Richland	Paved	22.9	7.9
18.	Bent Creek	Trail	16.1	9.8
19.	All Around Asheville	Paved	24.5	7.8
20.	Andrews Geyser	Mixed	9.6	6.1
21.	Craggy Gardens to Mount Mitchell Overlook	Paved	14.6	9.1
22.	Table Rock	Mixed	22.1	16.1
23.	Boone to Linn Cove	Paved	15.1	10.5
24.	Flatwoods	Dirt	18.6	6.2
25.	Doughton to Cumberland	Paved	23.7	11.2
26.	Virginia Creeper	Rail trail	18.0	13.3
27.	New River Trail	Rail trail	28.0	17.4

R: Road bike preferred
M: Mountain bike preferred
RT: Round-trip

EXTRA	TYPE	BIKE	HIGHLIGHTS
45.8	1-Way	R	Devils Courthouse and Richland Balsam
16.6	Loop	M	Fine singletrack and two-track
26.4	Loop	R	Hilltop views and neighborhoods
9.2	Loop	M	Andrews Geyser and old US 70
38.8	1-Way	R	Craggy Gardens and Mount Mitchell
49.0	Loop	M	Views of Linville Gorge
29.8	1-Way	R	Cone Manor and Linn Cove Viaduct
28.6	Loop	M	Views of Holston Mountain
47.4	1-Way	R	Brinegar Cabin and Fox Hunter Paradise
69.0	1-Way	M	Spectacular downhill riding
49.7	1-Way	M	Chestnut Creek and railroad tunnels

INTRODUCTION   Welcome to the world of bicycling in the mountains of the Southeast. The Blue Ridge and Smoky Mountains offer cyclists a wealth of fine riding areas. This guide aims to give you a taste of what the region offers, from paved scenic highways threading across high mountaintops to secluded singletrack trails snaking along rollicking creeks.

The 27 rides described here visit 23 top riding areas centered on the Blue Ridge Parkway and Great Smoky Mountains National Park. The guide includes rides in Georgia, Tennessee, North Carolina, and Virginia. Each ride is intended as an introduction to a specific area or trail network. However, in the case of the Blue Ridge Parkway, which covers 252 miles of the North Carolina high country, and the Tsali Recreation Area, where only half of the trails are open to riders each day, one ride per area just simply wasn't enough. The 27 rides are split evenly between paved roads suitable for road bikes and unpaved routes best suited to mountain bikes.

The rides fall easily into five groups. First are the scenic highways, which include the Blue Ridge Parkway, Cherohala Skyway, and Foothills Parkway in Great Smoky Mountains National Park. These rides are generally long one-way rides at high elevations on roads built for scenic driving. Traffic is usually light and relatively slow, and drivers are accustomed to sharing the road with bikes.

Expect lots of climbing on these routes; the roads were built with travel by auto in mind. But, there are numerous overlooks, picnic areas, and of course, unsurpassed views of the surrounding mountains. The payoff is high for your hard climbing.

The next group is more typical road rides. I've included loops near Asheville and Brevard, North Carolina, and Knoxville, Tennessee (House Mountain) that are favorites of local riders and well suited for out-of-towners. Two other paved loops (Cades Cove in Great Smoky Mountains National Park and the Chickamauga and Chattanooga National Military Park) circle some of the most historic landscapes in the national park system. Little River, near Townsend, Tennessee, and the Maryville-Alcoa Greenway are one-way rides. This group includes some of the easiest, most popular, and most scenic rides in the book.

Seven rides travel dirt roads or a combination of dirt and paved roads. These loops cover terrain suitable for beginning mountain bikers. Balsam Mountain–Cherokee, Jake Best–Doublecamp, and Andrews Geyser all have long climbs. There are can't-miss, out-and-back side trips to spectacular overlooks on the Cataloochee and

Hyatt Lane provides a quiet shortcut across Cades Cove in Great Smoky Mountains National Park

Table Rock rides. Flatwoods and Prentice Cooper are both under-utilized riding areas that serve as good practice for tougher riding areas. For all seven rides, your mountain bike is the right choice.

Four trail systems in the region were built with mountain biking in mind. These areas all have the wild and wooly singletrack that hard core riders want, but they also have more forgiving trails that are more than just a test of skill and stamina. Since your heart isn't in your throat, you're able to enjoy the scenery. The Ocoee and Chilhowee systems are relatively new trail systems built near the famous whitewater runs of the Ocoee River. The trail systems at Tsali and Bent Creek in North Carolina are the two best-known mountain biking destinations in the region. If you are unsure of your bike-handling skills, start with the Short and Sweet versions of these rides (see below).

Two superb rail trails in southwest Virginia justified extending the range of this guide north into the Commonwealth. The Virginia Creeper and New River Trails follow abandoned rail lines that have been converted to trails. Both are fantastic rides, suitable for the occasional rider but sufficiently scenic to please even the jaded veteran. There is no better way to see this beautiful countryside than on two wheels. Both trails have generated their own service industries as bike shops and shuttle services have sprung up to cater to the needs of cycling enthusiasts flocking to these traffic-free trails.

All of the rides described here are suitable for the average rider. But since none of us is really average, I've included two alternate versions of each ride. The Short and Sweet version hits the highlights but reduces the effort. These rides are a great alternative for family groups, less experienced riders, or anyone without a lot of time to spend on the bike. Remember that the Blue Ridge and Smokies are mountain ranges: Any riding here will require plenty of climbing.

On the opposite end of the spectrum are serious riders for whom the main routes will be just a springboard to greater adventure. For them, I've added the Extra Credit ride, a version long enough to feed their hunger for mileage and appetite for endorphins while keeping the scenery high caliber.

THE SOUTHERN APPALACHIAN MOUNTAINS   Great Smoky
Mountains National Park preserves the heart of the Southern
Appalachians' wild and rugged mountains. The park's 500,000
acres contain a rich cultural heritage and natural history unrivaled for its diversity and complexity. The Cades Cove and
Cataloochee areas are ideal for exploring by bike, and the adjacent Foothills Parkway offers fine riding as well. The leisurely
pace of cycling through the park opens your eyes to the richness
of life around you.

Extending north from the Smokies is the Blue Ridge Parkway,
a scenic highway managed by the National Park Service, that
extends for 469 miles to the Shenandoah National Park in
Virginia. Conceived to link the two great national parks of the
Southeast, the parkway has come into its own as a recreation destination. Its high impact scenery and bike-friendly management
make it one of the region's most popular draws for road bikers.
Here the hard work of hill climbing is rewarded with views of the
Blue Ridge's trademark endless layers of mountains.

Surrounding the Smokies and the Blue Ridge Parkway are over
a million acres of national forest lands. The Cherokee National
Forest extends north and south of the Smokies in Tennessee. In
North Carolina, the Nantahala National Forest to the south and
the Pisgah National Forest to the north surround the Smokies
and the Blue Ridge Parkway. In Virginia, the areas covered by
this guide are part of the George Washington and Jefferson
National Forests.

National forest lands are managed for a variety of uses ranging
from wilderness, where both motorized and mechanized vehicles
such as bicycles are not allowed, to recreation and timber produc-
tion. Several special areas within the forests present wonderful
cycling opportunities. The Mount Rogers National Recreation
Area, which includes part of the Virginia Creeper Trail, is managed by the Forest Service. The Chilhowee Recreation Area
(Cherokee National Forest) and the Tsali Recreation Area
(Nantahala National Forest) have great trails for hiking and biking. The Forest Service also manages the Bent Creek
Experimental Forest near Asheville, where recreation is just one

part of a complex group of management objectives. The Cherohala Skyway is managed cooperatively as a scenic highway by the Cherokee and Nantahala National Forests. Elsewhere, the huge network of paved and gravel roads managed by the Forest Service offers riders nearly limitless opportunities for exploration.

Outside of the national parks and forests are a number of other special places, such as the New River Trail State Park, which is operated by the Virginia Department of Conservation and Recreation. Most other state parks are too small to attract riders, but some, such as House Mountain near Knoxville, Tennesse, can be used as launching points for longer rides. The Chickamauga and Chattanooga National Military Park and Prentice Cooper State Forest and Wildlife Management Area are really part of the Cumberland Plateau, not the Southern Appalachians, but these two areas offer superb riding convenient to Chattanooga.

Both the North Carolina and Tennessee Departments of Transportation have established designated bike routes along state highways. This guide uses some of the bike routes in North Carolina along the Blue Ridge Parkway and near Brevard. Designated bike routes in Tennessee are not always well designed, and several appear likely to be extremely hazardous to cyclists. A few of the safer bike routes in east Tennessee are mentioned when they are close to those described in this guide. Please scout any of the others by car before trying to ride them.

WHEN TO RIDE   One of the great things about riding around the Blue Ridge and Smoky Mountains is the chance to get out your bike in all four seasons. Though all the riding areas described in this guide may be open year-round, it is important to check on riding conditions before heading out. The same factors that make the high mountains cool and alluring in summer can put them out of bounds in the winter months. The higher elevations of the Blue Ridge Parkway, Cherohala Skyway, and Foothills Parkway are often closed due to snow and ice in winter. Even when open in winter, any amount of snow and ice can make riding dangerous. In Great Smoky Mountains National Park, the roads leading into Cades Cove and Cataloochee are periodically closed due to winter weather. In order to avoid contaminating waterways, the park does not salt its roads in winter. Heintooga Ridge Road on the Balsam Mountain–Cherokee ride is closed to vehicles in winter but is always open to mountain bikers and foot travel.

Facilities for riders also are more limited in winter. Most campgrounds and picnic areas along the Blue Ridge Parkway and in Great Smoky Mountains National Park close for the season near the end of October. Don't plan on getting water or any other supplies at these areas without checking on their closure dates first. Many campgrounds and picnic areas operated by the Forest Service also close for the winter.

Like anywhere else, summer is the main riding season. The fast pace of riding (at least some of the time) helps cut through the heat and humidity that grips the summer air. But spring and fall also bring fine riding weather. Temperatures are milder, the days are still long, and you have the added bonus of spring's wildflower bonanza or fall's colorful leaves. Remember that weather in the mountains is wetter than that in the valleys below. A slight chance of rain in Knoxville, Asheville, or Chattanooga likely means you'll get wet in the high country.

The period between Memorial Day and Labor Day makes up the summer driving season. Traffic volume rises sharply as tourists flock to the mountains to escape the heat and enjoy the scenery. Likewise, weekends find roads and trails more heavily used, and holidays can be even more crowded. If you're concerned about traffic on a route, plan to start as early in the day as possible to avoid peak driving times. If you're riding in summer, an early start provides the added benefit of cooler temperatures. One exception to the early start rule is Cataloochee, where traffic is heavier near dusk and dawn as people arrive to watch the elk feed.

In Great Smoky Mountains National Park, Cades Cove Loop is closed to vehicles on Wednesday and Saturday mornings during summer. Without a doubt these are the best times to ride the loop. Auto traffic on the narrow winding road otherwise is amazingly heavy. The road is also closed to vehicles from dusk to dawn. If you miss the Wednesday or Saturday morning closures, your next best bet is to start as early as possible. Since half the fun of the ride is wildlife watching, and deer especially are most active early in the morning, this strategy can add significantly to your riding enjoyment.

In Prentice Cooper, riders should remember the area is closed to nonhunters on selected weekends in spring and fall. These closures are for hunts—not the weekends when you'd want to be riding anyway. Check the area's web site for these closure dates before heading out.

Tsali Recreation Area also has a unique trail schedule. On any particular day, half the trails are open to horseback riders and the other half are open to mountain bikers. At this time, Mouse Branch and Thompson Loops are open Tuesday, Thursday, and Saturday; while Left and Right Loops are open Monday, Wednesday, Friday, and Sunday. Though this schedule may change, there will always be a trail open to ride.

Mountain bikers should always avoid riding trails in wet or muddy conditions to avoid erosion. At Tsali, Bent Creek, Chilhowee, and Ocoee, the singletrack and old dirt roads can handle significant numbers of riders when the trails are dry, but these same trails can quickly deteriorate when wet. Please consider postponing your trip, finding some nice forest roads to ride, or going for a hike under these conditions.

There are a few annual events that may alter your riding plans. Tsali is the site of bike and multisport races several weekends a year. There are also races and a fat tire festival at Ocoee. The New River Trail may continue to host races. Events like these can be a great way to visit new riding areas, meet other riders, and test your skills. But if you are looking for a quiet weekend escape, it may be best to check the calendar for these areas before heading out.

USING THIS GUIDE   The information in the heading of each chapter provides important details concerning the rides. **Distance** is the first item and gives the length of the main ride, the Short and Sweet version, and the Extra Credit ride. Here you will also find out if the ride is a loop, a round trip, or a one-way ride, where a car shuttle will be needed.

Terrain describes just how hilly the ride will be and if the surface is paved roads, unpaved roads, or trails. If there are significant long climbs, these will also be described here. Paved roads are fine for touring bikes; for all other rides, I recommend using a mountain bike. Some riders prefer the lower gears of mountain bikes for very hilly rides such as the Blue Ridge Parkway or Cherohala Skyway. Here also you'll find the name of the park, forest, or organization that maintains the route. Contact information for these groups is in the Appendix.

Special Features describes the highlights of each ride. These range from historical sights and expansive overlooks to adrenaline-pumping downhills. **General Location** gives the direction and distance from the nearest town to the trailhead. **Maps** gives you a list of what other maps are available for the area.

Access provides detailed driving directions for the trailheads involved. To date, only the mountain-bike trail systems in the national forests and the New River Trail State Park are charging user fees. These fees are nominal, and the money goes directly to fund projects associated with the area. It is likely that other areas will eventually begin charging user fees, so don't assume that because a fee isn't mentioned in this guide, you will not be charged.

Each ride narrative begins with some background information about the route and the area. The ride description is given in cue sheet format, similar to the cue sheets many cycling groups use. Keep in mind that conditions on roads and trails are liable to change. The region's mountain-biking trail systems are all expanding in response to increasing use. While these changes yield more miles, they also yield more intersections and more opportunities to get lost.

When riding the roads, it's best to regard road signs as temporary phenomena. My home state of Tennessee seems particularly reluctant to let riders and drivers know where they are. Signage in national forests can also be undependable, especially just after fall hunting season.

At the end of the narrative are brief descriptions of two alternate versions of the main ride. The Short and Sweet version is a shorter, easier ride that still hits the highlights. The Extra Credit

ride is a longer, tougher ride that will appeal to more serious
cyclists. These added sections are a blatant attempt to make the
guide appeal to more riders. Rather than present just a few easy,
moderate, and difficult rides, all 27 rides are geared for a variety
of riding levels.

SAFETY, MAINTENANCE, AND REPAIR   The greatest hazard to
cyclists on any road is vehicles. Protecting yourself from vehicular
accidents should always be your first concern. Great care has been
taken to choose safe, low-traffic roads for this guide, but it only
takes one careless driver or rider to cause a collision. In this
region, few roads have shoulders, all but eliminating any margin
for error. The huge SUV's and monster motor homes popular these
days can occupy more than their share of the road, especially when
operated by inattentive or inexperienced drivers on winding
mountain roads.

To make it easy on drivers and to protect yourself, be sure to
follow all traffic regulations. Make yourself and your bike visible
with bright clothing and lights if necessary. In some places, it may
be necessary to pull over and wait before entering a tunnel or
crossing a major highway.

Besides vehicles, aggressive dogs are probably the next most
serious threat to cyclists. A scale of dog danger, similar to the
scale of difficulty that climbers and whitewater paddlers use, has
been developed for bicycle routes.

Class One: Dogs bring you a tasty treat
Class Two: Dogs ignore you
Class Three: Dogs bark but don't chase
Class Four: Dogs give chase but just for sport
Class Five: Doggie dental exam possible; evasive action necessary
Class Six: The dog's breath smells like your leg

Since most of these rides are on public land or greenways, the
level of dog danger is relatively low. Only House Mountain, part of
my riding route when I lived in that neighborhood, regularly rises
to class four. However, these dogs see few riders and aren't quite
sure how to handle us.

Should you encounter aggressive dogs, several courses of action are possible. A squirt with a water bottle is often enough to give you a little space. If they get really close, a swift kick will drive them away. Strangely, barking back also seems to work. You also can take the offensive. First, make sure the road is clear and then veer sharply toward the dog. Partly they like to chase, since you're running away anyway. If you look aggressive, they may think twice.

Keeping hydrated is essential, especially in the steamy heat of summer. Long climbs in the mountains and long road rides with little shade put riders in danger of running out of fluids. If you're not used to riding in this area or under these conditions, try to carry at least one extra bottle of water or a sports drink. Few of the rides in this guide, particularly those in the mountains or on remote trails, pass stores or vending machines. Assume any natural water supply you encounter is impure. No matter how hot the day or how thirsty you may be, do not drink any untreated water. One remedy is to carry iodine tablets and powdered drink mix (to mask the taste) with your emergency supplies. Even the road rides in this guide will pass through less populated areas. If you except to be out all day, pack accordingly.

Just as stores and supplies will be few, bike shops will be even fewer. There are fully equipped shops in larger towns such as Knoxville, Asheville, Chattanooga, Boone, and Cleveland, but none is directly on any of these routes. Only on the Virginia Creeper and New River Trails will you find bike shops along the route.

A few pieces of gear can make your riding much safer. Always wear a helmet, no matter what terrain you are riding on. Those sold in bike shops will protect better, have superior fit and ventilation, and last longer. Replace your helmet if it has been in a bad crash or is several years old. Bike gloves will both protect your hands in a fall and pad them against the wear and tear of bumpy trails.

Your repair kit should include a spare tube, a patch kit, tire irons, and a pump or inflation cartridge. Keep your chain lubed, especially in wet weather, and carry a chain tool in the event it breaks. Keeping your brakes and derailleur well tuned always pays off in more enjoyable riding.

GIVING BACK   You can create good will for other riders by following the rules of parks, forests, and roadways. Only on a few trail systems managed by the Forest Service are cyclists the dominant user group. In other places, on the highways especially, we are a small and vulnerable minority. Also, don't ride on trails closed to mountain bikers, and don't ride on any muddy trails.

You can help land managers by giving them constructive feedback on road or trail conditions. They genuinely appreciate hearing about problems in their area and surely can't fix things they don't know about. Just make sure to give them some positive feedback. Everyone likes to hear when they've done a good job.

Please support the local businesses that cater to cyclists and outdoor recreationists in general. These folks will appreciate your business and will more likely still be open when you really need that spare tube or box of energy bars. None of these folks is going to get rich selling gear or shuttling riders, so do what you can to keep these services alive.

First-time visitors to the Southeast are often appalled and amazed at the volume of roadside litter, but the carelessness of others is no excuse to be careless ourselves. Even though it may mean a little extra hassle, never litter. Take home everything you brought along. Even better, pitch in with a little cleanup work on a trail or at a trailhead. One rule of thumb is that places that start clean tend to stay that way, while places that are littered get worse fast.

Finally, if you like to ride on trails, pitch in and help with some trail work. You can find schedules for work days on the web sites of groups like the Chattanooga Bicycle Club or on Forest Service or Park Service web sites. Few things beat the satisfaction of riding on trail that you helped build or maintain.

RANKING THE RIDES   Not sure where to ride to escape from it all or where to go to meet some other avid riders? Here are a few subjective lists designed to help you find the ride that's right for you.

Most Popular

These rides are no secret, but there's good reason so many people love to ride them.

- Virginia Creeper
- New River Trail
- Maryville-Alcoa Greenway
- Bent Creek
- Cades Cove

Least Crowded

You can almost count on having these rides to yourself, at least until everyone else finds out about them.

- Flatwoods
- Jake Best–Doublecamp
- Table Rock
- House Mountain
- Balsam Mountain–Cherokee

Easiest Pedaling

Here's where to go when you want some easy cruising.

- Virginia Creeper
- New River Trail
- Maryville-Alcoa Greenway
- Cades Cove
- Chickamauga Battlefield

Hardest and Hilliest (Extra Credit rides)

Sometimes you need a challenge just to see what you're made of.

- Balsam Mountain–Cherokee
- Cherohala Skyway
- Pisgah to Richland (Blue Ridge Parkway)

- Boone to Linn Cove (Blue Ridge Parkway)
- Craggy Gardens to Mount Mitchell Overlook (Blue Ridge Parkway)

Best for Kids (Short and Sweet versions)

These rides are easy, scenic, and traffic free.

- Virginia Creeper
- New River Trail
- Maryville-Alcoa Greenway
- Chilhowee
- Chickamauga Battlefield

For Experienced Riders Only (Extra Credit rides)

These rides may include technical singletrack or use roads where traffic may be heavy.

- All Around Asheville
- Tsali Left Loop
- Bent Creek
- Brevard to Rosman
- Chilhowee

SOUTH
OF THE
SMOKIES

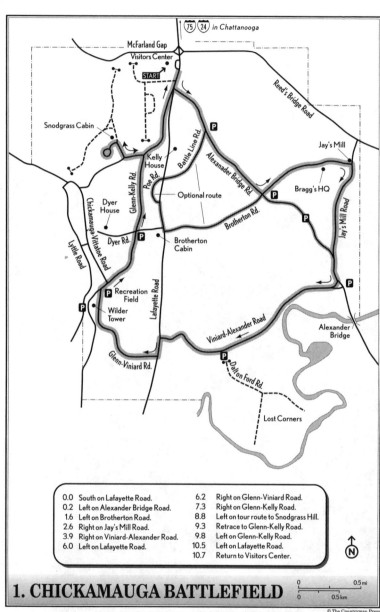

75 24 in Chattanooga

McFarland Gap
Visitors Center
START

Reed's Bridge Road

Snodgrass Cabin

Jay's Mill

Kelly House

Battle Line Rd.

Glenn-Kelly Rd.

Poe Rd.

Alexander Bridge Rd.

Bragg's HQ

Optional route

Dyer House

Brotherton Rd.

Jay's Mill Road

Chickamauga-Vitatoe Road

Dyer Rd.

Brotherton Cabin

Lyttle Road

Recreation Field

Lafayette Road

Wilder Tower

Viniard-Alexander Road

Alexander Bridge

Glenn-Viniard Rd.

Dalton Ford Rd.

Lost Corners

0.0	South on Lafayette Road.	6.2	Right on Glenn-Viniard Road.
0.2	Left on Alexander Bridge Road.	7.3	Right on Glenn-Kelly Road.
1.6	Left on Brotherton Road.	8.8	Left on tour route to Snodgrass Hill.
2.6	Right on Jay's Mill Road.	9.3	Retrace to Glenn-Kelly Road.
3.9	Right on Viniard-Alexander Road.	9.8	Left on Glenn-Kelly Road.
6.0	Left on Lafayette Road.	10.5	Left on Lafayette Road.
		10.7	Return to Visitors Center.

N

1. CHICKAMAUGA BATTLEFIELD

0   0.5 mi
0   0.5 km

© The Countryman Press

Chickamauga Battlefield

- **DISTANCE:** A 10.7-mile loop. The Short and Sweet version is a 7-mile loop. The Extra Credit ride is an 18-mile loop.
- **TERRAIN:** Level, paved roads within Chickamauga and Chattanooga National Military Park, which includes a short climb to Snodgrass Hill.
- **SPECIAL FEATURES:** Hundreds of monuments and interpretive sites commemorating this Civil War battlefield.
- **GENERAL LOCATION:** 7 miles south of Chattanooga, Tennessee.
- **MAPS:** Chickamauga and Chattanooga National Military Park Bicycle Guide. The pamphlet is available at the visitors center.
- **ACCESS:** From Exit 180B on I-24 in Chattanooga, drive 6.6 miles south on US 27 to the park boundary at Reed's Bridge Road. Continue straight on Lafayette Road for 0.2 mile to the visitors center. The park can also be reached in 7.9 miles from I-75 via GA 2 and Lafayette Road. During busy periods, park officials ask cyclists not to use the main visitors center parking area. For the closest parking alternatives on this loop, go to the small lot at the intersection of Lafayette and Alexander Bridge Roads at 0.2 mile or the larger lot near the junction of Battle Line and Alexander Bridge Roads at 0.6 mile.

The forests and farmlands west of Chickamauga Creek saw some of the bloodiest fighting of the Civil War. In September 1863, the Union Army of the Cumberland under General William

Rosecrans was marching toward Chattanooga intent on capturing this strategic railroad center. Hoping to surprise General Braxton Bragg's Confederate Army of Tennessee, Rosecrans tried to approach the city from the south. On September 19, Union and Confederate forces collided near Reed's Bridge. Fighting soon erupted into a confusing full-scale battle in the dense forests.

By nightfall, the two armies faced each other across Lafayette Road, now the main road through the park. Bragg planned a coordinated attack designed to cut off Union troops from Chattanooga. But Bragg's orders were confusing and the next day his troops moved too late. On the other side, Rosecrans had bad luck as well. Rosecrans was told one division was out of place along the front line, so he moved another to plug the hole. However, the first division was actually in the proper spot, so Rosecrans ended up creating a gap in the line by moving the other. The switch occurred

The Wilder Brigade Monument marks the site of the Union's stand on the pivotal day of fighting at Chickamauga.

just at the time and place where Confederate troops attacked. The Confederates poured across the Union line, and the Federal forces were nearly swept from the field in a disorderly retreat.

General George Thomas, later known as the Rock of Chickamauga for his stand, was able to hold Snodgrass Hill long enough for Union forces to reorganize and retreat north into Chattanooga. Of the 124,000 soldiers who fought at Chickamauga, nearly one in four was killed or wounded.

The Confederates besieged Union forces in Chattanooga through the fall of 1863. However, two armies reinforced the Union position, and combined with the arrival of General Ulysses Grant, provided enough firepower to defeat Bragg's troops in battles on Lookout Mountain, Orchard Knob, and Missionary Ridge. By November, nearly all of Tennessee was under Union control, and the route opened for General Sherman's march to Atlanta and the eventual end of the Civil War.

Nearly 12,000 veterans from both sides of the conflict attended a reunion at the battlefield in 1889. A bill to create the park was passed the next year, and the park was dedicated in 1895. Between 1893 and 1910, over 1,400 monuments and interpretive plaques were carefully placed to honor the bravery of the soldiers who fought here. The monuments left by the veterans precisely identify the key sites of the battle and offer visitors a unique insight into the ebb and flow of the fighting. A little time spent among the displays in the visitors center will help you get oriented and better appreciate the ride to come.

The leisurely pace of bike riding is ideal for exploring the Chickamauga's 5,300 acres. The history will add to the biking, and the biking will enhance the history. Though this ride is relatively short and the grades are easy, allow yourself plenty of time for exploration. Few parks anywhere offer the wealth of interpretive sites and monuments as does Chickamauga. It is unlikely a hardcore Civil War buff could see the entire battlefield in a day. Even the casual visitor will spend extra time taking advantage of this history lesson on the move.

The easy grades and gentle traffic of most park roads make it ideal for the casual cyclist and family groups. The wide bike lane on Glenn-Kelly Road is particularly good for family groups. Inside the park, only MacFarland Gap and Reed's Bridge Roads receive heavy vehicular traffic. The long-planned detour of US 27 around the park to the west and off Lafayette Road was completed in 2001. This has greatly reduced the volume and speed of traffic on Lafayette, making for safer riding. The park hopes to install a bike lane on Lafayette Road.

0.0 Leave the visitors center and ride south on Lafayette Road.

0.2 Turn left on Alexander Bridge Road by a small parking area.

0.6 Pass Battle Line Road on the right at another parking area.
Battle Line Road marks the front where the bulk of the opposing armies met on the second day of the fighting. Here Confederate armies under General Polk faced Union troops under General Thomas. Most of the units stationed here chose to place their commemorative monuments at their original positions, so the road contains more monuments per mile than any other battlefield road. One of the most interesting is a giant acorn, the symbol of the Union Army of the Cumberland.

In 0.5 mile, you will pass a side trail on the right that leads to one of the few marked graves on the battlefield, that of Private John Ingraham, a local soldier buried by his neighbors.

1.6 Turn left at the intersection on Brotherton Road.
There is a parking lot and picnic area at this intersection. The junction was the site of the last major attack on September 19, 1863. Bragg's overnight headquarters was located about 0.5 mile down Brotherton Road.

2.6 Turn right at the intersection with Jay's Mill Road.
It was near Jay's Mill Bridge that Union infantry first encountered Confederate calvary to ignite the two-day battle. Because the Confederate troops quickly pushed the Union army west, you will notice fewer monuments along this road. Today, the road is an example of a different type of conflict. Pine trees along the road have been devastated by the Southern pine beetle, a small insect that bores into mature trees, eventually killing them.

3.6 Pass an intersection with Alexander Bridge Road on the right.

3.9 Turn right on Viniard-Alexander Road.
Alexander's Bridge site is 0.4 mile ahead on the left fork.

5.3 Pass the gravel Dalton Ford Road and a parking area on the left.
*Those with mountain bikes can take the 1.1-mile, one-way trip to the Lost Corners
area of the park by bearing right at the road's first intersection. The unpaved road
lined with mature trees gives the sense of stepping back in history.*

6.0 Turn left on Lafayette Road.

6.2 Turn right on Glenn-Viniard Road and proceed with traffic along this one-
way road.
*Just before reaching the next intersection, pass a parking area for Wilder Brigade
Monument, the battlefield's most impressive tribute. This 85-foot-tall limestone
structure sits atop the small hill used by Rosecrans as his headquarters and later
held by Wilder's brigade on September 20th, before the retreat of the Union army
into Chattanooga.*

7.3 Turn right on Glenn-Kelly Road.
There is a designated bike lane on the left side of the road.

7.4 Pass an intersection with Chickamauga-Vittatoe Road branching left.
The park's recreation fields are to your right.

8.1 Cross Dyer Road.
*It was near the junction of Dyer Road that Confederate troops poured through the
gap in the Union lines, leading to the rout of Federal forces. The Lee Dyer House to
the left was built in 1875.*

8.8 Turn left to follow the tour route to Snodgrass Hill, the ride's only hill.
*The tiny cabin was used as a field hospital during the fierce fighting around
Snodgrass Hill. The hill, with a commanding view of the surrounding countryside,
was where Union forces under General Thomas were finally able to make a stand
after their lines were shattered by the Confederate advance. The array of cannons
and monuments on the hill are evidence of the desperate fighting that occurred
here. Be sure to continue past the cabin to the dense grove of monuments on the
hilltop.*

9.3 Retrace your route back to Glenn-Kelly Road.

9.8 Turn left on Glenn-Kelly Road.

10.5 Turn left on Lafayette Road.

10.7 Return to the visitors center parking area.

Short and Sweet: Follow the park's auto tour route for a 7-mile loop. The park may change the current route.

For Extra Credit: Add a second loop down the monument-filled Battle Line Road to Lafayette and then take Brotherton and Alexander Bridge Roads to the Jay's Mill Road intersection. Next follow the main loop in reverse back to the visitors center for an 18.0-mile loop.

2

Prentice Cooper

- **DISTANCE:** A 15.2-mile loop with a side trip. The Short and Sweet version is a 10.2-mile loop. The Extra Credit ride adds a longer side trip to total 27.2 miles.

- **TERRAIN:** Rolling jeep trails and dirt roads in Prentice Cooper State Forest and Wildlife Management Area, which includes one 300-foot hill.

- **SPECIAL FEATURES:** Snoopers Rock Overlook above the Tennessee River Gorge.

- **GENERAL LOCATION:** About 10 miles west of Chattanooga, Tennessee.

- **MAPS:** A map of Prentice Cooper State Forest and Wildlife Management Area is available from the Tennessee Wildlife Resources Foundation.

- **ACCESS:** The trickiest part of this drive is sorting out the different roads through Chattanooga with the number 27. From I-75 in downtown Chattanooga, take Exit 178 onto US 27N. In 4.8 miles, split off to the left onto US 127. In another 1.9 miles, turn left on TN 27 at a sign for Prentice Cooper. In 8.2 miles, at the rim of the Cumberland Plateau, turn left at another PRENTICE COOPER sign. Continue to follow the signs, making a left turn in 0.1 mile, then another left on Game Reserve Road in 0.2 mile. Enter Prentice Cooper by going straight at the stop sign in 0.1 mile on the gravel Tower Road. Once into the area it is 0.7 mile to the entrance station and another 0.3 mile to a parking area at the junction with Persimmon Branch Road.

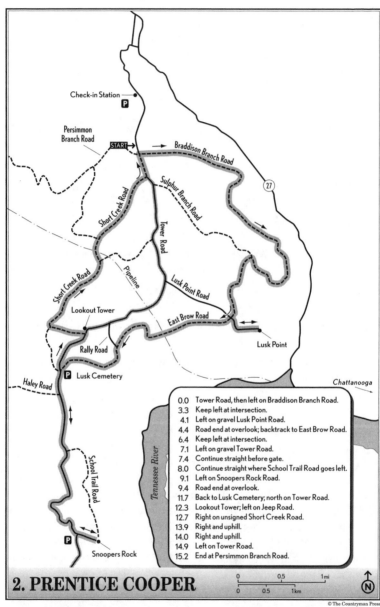

Check-in Station
P

Persimmon
Branch Road

START→ Braddison Branch Road

Short Creek Road

Sulphur Branch Road

Tower Road

Short Creek Road

Pipeline

Lusk Point Road

Lookout Tower

East Brow Road

Rally Road

Lusk Point

P Lusk Cemetery

Haley Road

Chattanooga

School Trail Road

Tennessee River

P

Snoopers Rock

0.0 Tower Road, then left on Braddison Branch Road.
3.3 Keep left at intersection.
4.1 Left on gravel Lusk Point Road.
4.4 Road end at overlook; backtrack to East Brow Road.
6.4 Keep left at intersection.
7.1 Left on gravel Tower Road.
7.4 Continue straight before gate.
8.0 Continue straight where School Trail Road goes left.
9.1 Left on Snoopers Rock Road.
9.4 Road end at overlook.
11.7 Back to Lusk Cemetery; north on Tower Road.
12.3 Lookout Tower; left on Jeep Road.
12.7 Right on unsigned Short Creek Road.
13.9 Right and uphill.
14.0 Right and uphill.
14.9 Left on Tower Road.
15.2 End at Persimmon Branch Road.

0   0.5   1mi
0   0.5   1km

N

2. PRENTICE COOPER

© The Countryman Press

Prentice Cooper State Forest and Wildlife Management Area, perched on the edge of the Cumberland Plateau, is a wonderful recreation resource just north of Chattanooga. The 23,000-acre area contains a number of jeep roads that are ideal for exploring on a mountain bike. Wildlife watching and the spectacular overlooks above the Tennessee River Gorge make this an area worth visiting in all four seasons. The area sits on a high forested plateau above a deep gorge that is known as the Grand Canyon of Tennessee.

Prentice Cooper is a multiuse area. It is closed to recreation users on four weekends during the fall for deer hunting and on some weekends for spring turkey hunts. Check the area web site for closures before you ride. The area is also closed from dusk to dawn. Primitive camping is allowed at first-come, first-served sites at the check-in station and at Davis Pond on Tower Road.

Thirty miles of Tennessee's Cumberland Trail State Park also cross the area, but this trail is closed to mountain bikers. Of most concern to mountain bikers will be ATV use in the area. Prentice Cooper is the only ride in this guide where bikes will share a route with these motorized vehicles. ATV use means that some trails are eroded and rutted, and your ride can occasionally be noisily interrupted. But in general, conflicts between nonmotorized and motorized users are few.

Navigating Prentice Cooper can be a bit tricky. Tower Road is well maintained, and sturdy wooden posts mark all intersecting roads; but secondary roads are not marked, except at their intersection with Tower Road. There are numerous less-traveled trails not shown on any maps. The riding described here covers both jeep roads and the well-maintained Tower Road. The jeep roads are mostly wide and hills are usually short. This is a good area for those looking to expand their riding skills beyond rail trails and forest service roads and for those learning how to ride more technical trails. A little taste of Prentice Cooper can build a hunger for more off-road riding.

0.0 Ride south on Tower Road and turn left on Braddison Branch Road.
This dirt and packed sand road is typical of the jeep roads at Prentice Cooper, and

The Tennessee River and Raccoon Mountain dominate the view from Snoopers Rock.

the rides on the Cumberland Plateau in general. The road becomes more eroded as it approaches the rim of the Tennessee River Gorge. The toughest spot is a steep and rocky descent to a crossing of a small stream.

3.3 Keep left at the unmarked intersection with Sulphur Branch Road.
The left fork is East Brow Road. You will pass one old road on the right, which is blocked by a cable, and make another rocky crossing of a small stream.

4.1 Turn left at the unsigned intersection with the graveled Lusk Point Road.

4.4 Reach Lusk Point Overlook at the road's end.
The overlook is overgrown but still offers views of the Tennessee River. The Cumberland Trail is just below. Ride back up the hill to East Brow Road past the first intersection of Lusk Point and Brow Roads.

4.7 The unsigned intersection with the second leg of East Brow Road is just 100 yards past the intersection with the first leg.

5.4 Cross a pipeline corridor.

6.4 Keep left at the intersection with unsigned Rally Road.
Just beyond the intersection is a wildlife opening and the start of the signed Cemetery Loop.

7.1 Turn left on the gravel Tower Road at Lusk Cemetery.
The cemetery contains graves as recent as 2001.

7.4 Continue straight, just before a gate where Haley Road turns right.

8.0 Continue straight where School Trail Road goes left.
You could use School Trail Road as a rougher alternate route to Snoopers Rock.

8.3 The intersection with Sheep Rock Road on the right marks the start of a 300-foot drop.

9.1 Turn left on Snoopers Rock Road at a parking area, picnic area, and trail-head for the Cumberland Trail.

9.4 Reach parking for Snoopers Rock Overlook.
The road ends just before the overlook at the intersection with School Trail Road and the Cumberland Trail. Leave your bike here and walk 100 yards or so to the overlook. The name Snoopers dates back to Prohibition, when revenuers used the overlook to spot the small fires of moonshiners working in the valley below. The rock sits at the head of the oxbow bend of the Tennessee River around Raccoon Mountain.

11.7 Retrace your route back to Lusk Cemetery and continue north on Tower Road.

12.3 Reach the Prentice Cooper maintenance area and Lookout Tower.
The tower is one of the few in the state system still open to the public, though the cab is locked. The view from the upper levels includes Raccoon Mountain but not the river. Climb the tower at your own risk.
*   To continue the ride, turn left off Tower Road on a jeep road leading through the maintenance area.*

12.7 Turn right on the unsigned Short Creek Road.
Ignore a dirt road that soon enters on the left. Short Creek Road is a bit rougher than the jeep trails east of Tower Road. Cross one small stream, then a larger one followed by a short steep climb.

13.7 Go straight at a parking area where the unsigned gravel Natural Bridge Road enters on the right.
To the left, a path leads to a small pond.

13.9 Go right and uphill at an intersection with a road blocked by a cable.
The pipeline corridor also intersects the road at this point.

14.0 Go right and uphill where unsigned Maple Branch Road goes left along the contour.

14.9 Turn left on Tower Road.

15.2 End at the junction with Persimmon Branch Road.

Short and Sweet: From Lusk Cemetery, shortcut back to the trailhead via the well-graded Tower Road for a 10.2-mile loop.

For Extra Credit: Extend your side trip for 6 miles to the south end of Tower Road for a 27.2-mile loop. Or, from the trailhead, continue on Maple Branch Road to the popular ride on Persimmon Branch Road.

3

Ocoee

- **DISTANCE:** An 8.3-mile loop. The Short and Sweet version is a 6-mile loop. The Extra Credit ride is 17.9 miles.

- **TERRAIN:** The trails are a mix of two-track dirt roads and moderate singletrack trails in the Ocoee Ranger District of the Cherokee National Forest. There is a 300-foot climb at the start.

- **SPECIAL FEATURES:** Fun riding on a brand-new trail system next to the Ocoee Whitewater Center.

- **GENERAL LOCATION:** About 30 miles east of Cleveland, Tennessee.

- **MAPS:** Trails Illustrated Tellico and Ocoee Rivers, Cherokee National Forest, TN #781. The Chattanooga Bicycle Club web site may have the most up-to-date and accurate map.

- **ACCESS:** The Ocoee Whitewater Center is located on US 64, 6.3 miles west of the junction of US 64 and TN 68, and 20.9 miles east of the overpass on US 64 above US 411. The center is a fee area. In 2002, parking was $3 per day. There is short-term metered parking in front of the center and day-use parking farther downstream. Concrete walkways on both sides of the river lead from the parking area to the center. There is a large pedestrian bridge over the Ocoee on the east side of the center. Old Copper Road Trail begins on the north side of the bridge, and Bear Paw Loop begins on the south side of the bridge.

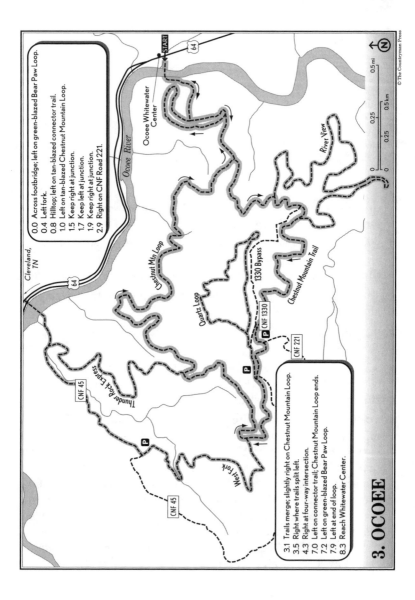

Cleveland, TN

Ocoee River

Ocoee Whitewater Center

River View

START

64

64

CNF 45

CNF 45

Thunder Rock Express

West Fork

Chestnut Mtn Loop

Quartz Loop

1330 Bypass

P CNF 1330

P

CNF 221

Chestnut Mountain Trail

0.0 Across footbridge; left on green-blazed Bear Paw Loop.
0.4 Left fork.
0.8 Hilltop; left on tan-blazed connector trail.
1.0 Left on tan-blazed Chestnut Mountain Loop.
1.5 Keep right at junction.
1.7 Keep left at junction.
1.9 Keep right at junction.
2.9 Right on CNF Road 221.

3.1 Trails merge; slightly right on Chestnut Mountain Loop.
3.5 Right where trails split left.
4.3 Right at four-way intersection.
7.0 Left on connector trail; Chestnut Mountain Loop ends.
7.2 Left on green-blazed Bear Paw Loop.
7.9 Left at end of loop.
8.3 Reach Whitewater Center.

N

0   0.25   0.5 mi
0   0.25   0.5 km

© The Countryman Press

3. OCOEE

The Ocoee River basin is in the process of a remarkable transformation from a landscape stripped bare of its natural features to a mecca for outdoor recreation. Just to the east, around the community of Ducktown, 140 years of copper mining and smelting left a denuded valley laced with pits and mining shafts. Logging to provide timbers for the mines and fuel for the smelters stripped the surroundings bare. Decades of acid discharge long prevented the recovery of the forests. In addition, the Ocoee River was dammed in three places between 1912 and 1941 to provide badly needed hydroelectric power.

Now, however, much of the basin is recovering. Since the last copper mine closed in 1987, all but the largest mining pits in Ducktown are at least partly revegetated. The surrounding forests are also recovering. On the north side of the river is the 4,700-acre Little Frog Wilderness. On the south side of the river, and adjacent to the mountain biking trails, is Big Frog Wilderness. Big Frog, together with Georgia's adjacent Cohutta Wilderness, is the largest protected wilderness in the Southern Appalachians.

The Ocoee River has long been one of the Southeast's legendary whitewater runs, famous for its sustained technical sections, year-round availability, and easy road access. The river's highest honor came when it was chosen as the site for the whitewater events during the 1996 Atlanta Summer Olympics. The Ocoee River below Ocoee Powerhouse #2 was the popular whitewater run, but event organizers soon realized the potential of an unused section of the river below Ocoee Dam #3. Because most river water was diverted from the channel directly to Ocoee Power Station #3, this section was not an established run but could be modified to suit the needs of the competition.

Using the natural characteristics of the river as much as possible, the Cherokee National Forest, Tennessee Valley Authority (TVA), and the Olympic Committee were able to construct a scenic and challenging course fit for Olympians. In fact, the course was so popular that TVA was soon pressured to open the course for recreational runs at the expense of its commercial power generation. A compromise was reached, and TVA now diverts water from

Ocoee Powerhouse #3 to the river for whitewater enthusiasts on 20 weekend days a year.

The 1996 Atlanta Summer Olympics had a huge long-term impact on the Ocoee area. The facilities from the games are now the Cherokee National Forest's Ocoee Whitewater Center. The Forest Service expanded the recreation options around the river by beginning construction on the new Tanasi Trail system. In 1998, Old Copper Road Trail and Bear Paw Loop were opened. These trails were built for multiple users, including mountain bikers, horseback riders, and hikers. Next to be built was Chestnut Mountain Loop, which gave the area enough trail miles to start attracting mountain bikers.

In 2001, the Cherokee National Forest completed an expansion of the Tanasi Trail system by adding four new trails (River View, 1330 Bypass, Quartz Loop, and Thunder Rock Express). In 2002 the Cherokee National Forest added a 1.5-mile paved connector trail alongside US 64 from Ocoee Powerhouse #3 to the Ocoee Whitewater Center. Another 6.7 miles of trails east of Boyd Gap and south of US 64 was added the same year. Expect that the Cherokee National Forest will continue to expand this trail system. The route described here begins at the Ocoee Whitewater Center and follows Bear Paw and Chestnut Mountain Loops.

0.0 From the Ocoee Whitewater Center, cross the footbridge above the river and turn left on the green-blazed Bear Paw Loop.
Bear Paw Loop will follow the river upstream and then turn right to climb steadily beside a small stream.

0.4 Where the trail forks, bear left to follow the loop clockwise.

0.8 At the top of the hill, turn left to start the tan-blazed connector trail between Bear Paw and Chestnut Mountain Loops.

1.0 Bear left at the start of Chestnut Mountain Loop.
Chestnut Mountain Loop here is a wide, tan-blazed two-track road called Cherokee National Forest (CNF) Road 1330.

1.5 Keep right at the junction with the blue-blazed River View Trail.
River View is one of the more difficult trails in the system. Adding this loop to your ride will extend your distance by 3 miles and considerably extend your workout.

A footbridge over the Ocoee River commemorating the 1996 Summer Olympic Games marks the start of the Ocoee trail system.

1.7 Keep left at the junction with the orange-blazed 1330 Bypass Trail.
If singletrack is your thing, the 1330 Bypass Trail will join Chestnut Mountain Loop near the junction with CNF Road 221. Taking 1330 Bypass Trail shortens the loop by 0.3 mile.

1.9 Keep right where River View Trail rejoins the loop.

2.9 1330 Bypass Trail rejoins the loop within site of a gate across CNF Road 1330 at its intersection with CNF Road 221. Turn right on CNF Road 221.
There is a pullout here, which may be signed CHESTNUT MOUNTAIN TRAILHEAD.

3.1 Reach the West Fork Trailhead on CNF Road 221.
Several trails merge at this important junction. To the left West Fork Trail (also part of Benton MacKaye Trail) leads south into Big Frog Wilderness. This trail is open to foot travel only. Straight ahead, CNF Road 221 leads to CNF Road 45 in 0.5 mile. Heading sharply right is the singletrack start of Quartz Loop, which could add 2.2 miles to your ride. Our route goes gently right to follow Chestnut Mountain Loop along the same route as the combined West Fork and Benton MacKaye Trails. The trails lead north down an old road that formerly was part of CNF Road 45.

3.5 Turn right where the trails split off left and Chestnut Mountain Loop follows CNF Road 33641.
This segment may also be signed LOOP C. Enjoy as fast, smooth descent.

4.3 Bear right at a four-way intersection where the green-blazed Thunder Rock Express Trail leads left and an abandoned logging road continues straight ahead.
Adrenaline junkies with good climbing skills will love the fast technical singletrack on the descent of Thunder Rock Express. Most riders descend Thunder Rock Express, turn left to climb up CNF Road 45 for 0.9 mile to the CNF Road 45 Trailhead, and then bear left to continue 1.2 miles up the combined West Fork and Benton MacKaye Trails to rejoin the loop at the 3.5-mile junction.

Beyond the Thunder Rock Express junction, Chestnut Mountain Loop narrows to easy singletrack across steep slopes covered with a healthy second growth forest. Rolling grades and pretty forest make this section a favorite of area regulars. Pass intersections with two spur roads.

7.0 Bear left on the connector between Bear Paw and Chestnut Mountain Loops at the end of Chestnut Mountain Loop.

7.2 Turn left to follow the green-blazed Bear Paw Loop.
The scenic side of Bear Paw Loop offers views across the Ocoee River to Little Frog Wilderness. A bench marks the site of commanding views down to the river and the Ocoee Whitewater Center.

7.9 Turn left at the end of the loop and retrace your inbound route.

8.3 Reach the trailhead at the Ocoee Whitewater Center.

Short and Sweet: If you'd like a shorter loop that avoids the climb from the Ocoee River to the Chestnut Mountain Loop, start your ride at the West Fork Trailhead. To reach the West Fork Trailhead, drive gravel CNF Road 45 past Thunder Rock Campground for 3.0 miles to the junction with CNF Road 221. Turn left on CNF Road 221 to reach the West Fork Trailhead in 0.5 mile.

For Extra Credit: By combining River View Trail (adds 3 miles), Quartz Loop (adds 2.2 miles), and the loop using Thunder Rock Express, CNF Road 45, and West Fork Trail (adds 4.4 miles), riders can cover almost the entire trail system in one 17.9-mile day.

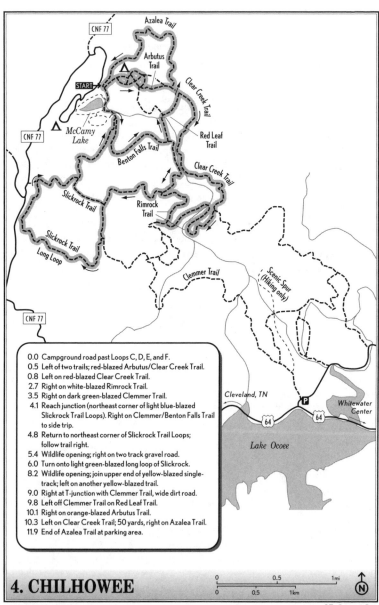

Azalea *Trail*

CNF 77

Arbutus
Trail

START

Clear Creek Trail

Red Leaf
Trail

CNF 77

*McCamy
Lake*

Benton Falls Trail

Clear Creek Trail

Slickrock Trail

Rimrock
Trail

Slickrock Trail

Long Loop

Clemmer Trail

Scenic Spur
(Hiking only)

CNF 77

Cleveland, TN

0.0 Campground road past Loops C, D, E, and F.
0.5 Left of two trails; red-blazed Arbutus/Clear Creek Trail.
0.8 Left on red-blazed Clear Creek Trail.
2.7 Right on white-blazed Rimrock Trail.
3.5 Right on dark green-blazed Clemmer Trail.
4.1 Reach junction (northeast corner of light blue-blazed Slickrock Trail Loops). Right on Clemmer/Benton Falls Trail to side trip.
4.8 Return to northeast corner of Slickrock Trail Loops; follow trail right.
5.4 Wildlife opening; right on two track gravel road.
6.0 Turn onto light green-blazed long loop of Slickrock.
8.2 Wildlife opening; join upper end of yellow-blazed single-track; left on another yellow-blazed trail.
9.0 Right at T-junction with Clemmer Trail, wide dirt road.
9.8 Left off Clemmer Trail on Red Leaf Trail.
10.1 Right on orange-blazed Arbutus Trail.
10.3 Left on Clear Creek Trail; 50 yards, right on Azalea Trail.
11.9 End of Azalea Trail at parking area.

P

Whitewater
Center

Lake Ocoee

64   64

4. CHILHOWEE

0   0.5   1mi
0   0.5   1km

N

Chilhowee

- **DISTANCE:** An 11.9-mile loop. The Short and Sweet version is a 3.6-mile loop. The Extra Credit ride is a 16.1-mile loop with a long climb.
- **TERRAIN:** A good mixture of singletrack trails and old two-track roads in Chilhowee Recreation Area (Cherokee National Forest).
- **SPECIAL FEATURES:** Benton Falls and Clemmer Trail.
- **GENERAL LOCATION:** 23 miles east of Cleveland, Tennessee.
- **MAPS:** Trails Illustrated Tellico and Ocoee Rivers, Cherokee National Forest, TN #781. The Chattanooga Bicycle Club web site may have a more up-to-date and accurate map.
- **ACCESS:** From the US 411 overpass on US 64 east of Cleveland, drive 7.5 miles east on US 64, just past the Ocoee Ranger Station, to Cherokee National Forest (CNF) Road 77. Turn left on the paved CNF Road 77. Drive 7.7 miles up Chilhowee Mountain and make a right turn into Chilhowee Recreation Area. In 0.4 mile the road will split. Take the left fork and drive 0.2 mile to the day-use parking area where there is a map board and pay station.

A long with the mountain bike trails near the Ocoee Whitewater Center, Chilhowee Recreation Area has one of the newer trail systems in the Cherokee National Forest. Both trail systems are designed for, and used primarily by, mountain bikers. Both are systems of front-country trails that partly incorporate previously existing road systems and are easily accessible from established campgrounds, making them easier for the Forest Service to maintain than trails deep in the backcountry. Part of the Chilhowee trail system has been in place since the early 1990s, but the Slickrock Trail Loops are relatively new additions to the system.

All but two of the Chilhowee trails are open to mountain bikers. The Chilhowee Forest Walk, on the south shore of McCamy Lake, is open to foot travel only. On the TN 30 side, Scenic Spur Trail is also open to foot travel only. Please respect these closures, even if the signs indicating them are not in place. Also be aware that the trails leading to Benton Falls are popular with hikers, and that you should yield the trail to them if necessary. Benton Falls, Arbutus, Red Leaf, and Azalea Trails are suitable for beginners and families, so you should control your speed close to the campground and near McCamy Lake.

First-time riders at Chilhowee may be dazzled, or dazed, by the web of trails leading from the day-use parking area. Take a good long look at the map board by the pay station and remember that Slickrock Loop and Azalea Spur Trails are not shown on this otherwise excellent map. You can think of the trails as a complicated loop between the upper trailhead at the recreation area and the lower trailhead on TN 30. Clear Creek Trail forms the northeast leg of the loop, while Slickrock and Clemmer Trails form the southwest leg. The trails have color-coded blazes, but several trail sections (particularly Clemmer and Benton Falls) have more than one trail name.

This chapter describes a difficult 11.9-mile figure 8. The first and longer loop connects Clear Creek, Rimrock, Slickrock Loop, and Clemmer Trails. The second and shorter loop follows Azalea Trail. The most difficult part of the ride is the 1-mile Rimrock Trail, which drops into, then climbs out of, the Rock Creek Gorge. However, the opportunities for making your own route here are nearly endless, and the ride offers four places to bail out. Though most of the riding throughout the trail system is fine for experienced riders, if you travel Clear Creek Trail beyond the junction with Rimrock Trail, or Clemmer Trail beyond the last junction

Riders will find the Chilhowee Trails well-marked and newcomer-friendly.

with Slickrock Loop Trail, you will be riding 1,000 feet down to TN 30 and back up.

0.0 From the day-use parking area, ride down the campground road past Loops C, D, E, and F.
For those looking to ride for an entire weekend, the campground offers quiet, spacious sites, low occupancy, modern bathhouses, and swimming in McCamy Lake.

0.5 At the far end of the campground, take the red-blazed Arbutus and Clear Creek Trails, which follow the left of two trails leaving from the end of the loop.

0.7 Pass Azalea Spur Trail (CNF Trail 140A) on the left.
Azalea Spur leads back to the campground at Loop E.

0.8 Pass Azalea Trail (CNF Trail 140) on the left.
In 50 yards the orange-blazed Arbutus Trail will split off right, continuing to follow the wide roadbed. Turn left on the narrower red-blazed Clear Creek Trail. Clear Creek is gently rolling and crosses two wooden bridges, one with a ramp for bikes

and one without. The trail will approach the Rock Creek Gorge, then turns left to follow the rim.

2.7 Turn right on the white-blazed Rimrock Trail where Clear Creek Trail turns left to reach TN 30 in 3.1 miles.

Rimrock Trail is the most difficult part of this ride. The trail starts out as an old road but soon turns into a slide-the-butt-back, clamp-on-the-brakes descent over a succession of whoop-de-dos. Halfway through, cross the creek and then struggle to gain back all your elevation. The creek crossing is a good point to gauge whether there is enough water in Rock Creek to justify the side trip to Benton Falls.

3.5 Turn right on the dark green-blazed Clemmer Trail, which follows a wide sandy roadbed.

4.1 Reach a junction with the northeast corner of the light blue-blazed Slickrock Loop Trail (CNF Trail 4032).

To visit Benton Falls, or take the shortcut #1 back to the trailhead, turn right and follow the Clemmer and Benton Falls trails to a signed junction above the falls.

4.45 Reach the side trail to Benton Falls.

The side trail is too steep to ride but is well worth the short walk. The 70-foot falls drops down a sheer rock face. Late in the year water flows can be very low. Shortcut #1 reaches the parking area in 1.5 miles via Benton Falls Trail.

4.8 Return to the northeast corner of the Slickrock Loop Trail.

This time follow the Slickrock Trail that now leads to the right.

5.4 In a weedy wildlife opening, bear right to follow a two-track gravel road.

Though tough for mountain bikers to navigate in summer, these openings provide crucial wildlife forage. Watch for wild turkey in the woods around the opening.

5.5 A yellow-blazed singletrack trail leads right.

This 0.45-mile connector trail is shortcut #2, which allows you to skip the long loop of Slickrock, probably the most rugged part of this ride. Shortcut #2 shaves 2.2 miles off the ride but is rocky with plenty of tree roots.

6.0 Turn right off the gravel road on the light-green-blazed long loop of Slickrock Loop Trail.

Begin a 0.5-mile climb here and then enter a rocky section. After passing two wooden bridges, the trail climbs up and over a knob of blocky sandstone.

7.7 Gated two-track CNF Road 33-0902 joins from the left, within sight of CNF Road 77.

8.2 At another wildlife opening, join the upper end of the yellow-blazed singletrack connector, which serves as shortcut #2.
Turn left here on another yellow-blazed trail, which is part of the Slickrock Loop Trail.

9.0 Turn right at a T-junction with Clemmer Trail, which follows a wide smooth dirt road.
At this junction, shortcut #3 turns left to follow a blue-blazed trail back to the day-use parking area in 0.3 mile.

9.8 Turn left off Clemmer Trail on Red Leaf Trail.
A right turn at this junction will lead 0.4 mile to Benton Falls.

10.1 Turn right on the orange-blazed Arbutus Trail.
A left turn here will lead to the end of the campground in 0.6 mile.

10.3 Turn left on Clear Creek Trail.
You can follow Clear Creek back to the campground in 0.3 mile for shortcut #4.
*   In 50 yards turn right on Azalea Trail. Azalea is wide singletrack with little elevation gain but enough rocks and roots to keep the riding interesting.*

11.0 Pass a junction on the right with the well-defined CNF Road 33-571.

11.9 Reach the end of Azalea Trail at the day-use parking area.

Short and Sweet: Riders uncomfortable with singletrack or rough trails should stick to Benton Falls, Azalea, Arbutus, and Red Leaf Trails. These trails can be combined into a 3.6-mile loop from the day-use parking area that includes the side trip to Benton Falls.

For Extra Credit: Serious riders will want to challenge themselves by adding Clemmer and Clear Creek Trails from TN 30. Joining this route at the long loop of Slickrock and leaving at the junction with Rimrock and Clear Creek Trails makes a 16.1-mile loop with 1,000 feet of elevation gain.

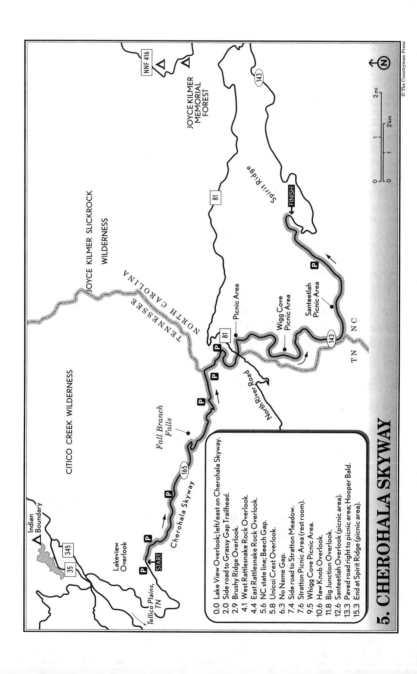

5. CHEROHALA SKYWAY

0.0 Lake View Overlook; left/east on Cherohala Skyway.
2.0 Side road to Grassy Gap Trailhead.
2.9 Brushy Ridge Overlook.
4.1 West Rattlesnake Rock Overlook.
4.4 East Rattlesnake Rock Overlook.
5.6 NC state line; Beech Gap.
5.8 Unicoi Crest Overlook.
6.3 No Name Gap.
7.4 Side road to Stratton Meadow.
7.6 Stratton Picnic Area (rest room).
9.5 Whigg Cove Picnic Area.
10.6 Haw Knob Overlook.
11.8 Big Junction Overlook.
12.6 Santeetlah Overlook (picnic area).
13.3 Paved road right to picnic areas; Hooper Bald.
15.3 End at Spirit Ridge (picnic area).

Cherohala Skyway

- **DISTANCE:** 15.3 miles one way. The Short and Sweet version is 9.7 miles one way, and the Extra Credit ride is 29 miles one way.

- **TERRAIN:** A paved one-way ride with continuous hills, including a net climb of 1,800 feet. The Skyway is jointly administered by the Cherokee and Nantahala National Forests.

- **SPECIAL FEATURES:** This is perhaps the most scenic mountain ride in the Southeast.

- **GENERAL LOCATION:** About 20 miles east of Tellico Plains, Tennesse.

- **MAPS:** Cherokee and Nantahala National Forest Cherohala Skyway (this brochure is available from Forest Service Offices) and Trails Illustrated Tellico and Ocoee Rivers, Cherokee National Forest, TN #781.

- **ACCESS:** From the junction of TN 68 and TN 165 in Tellico Plains, drive east on TN 165, which becomes the Cherohala Skyway outside of town. At 5.3 miles, pass a junction with Cherokee National Forest (CNF) Road 210, which leads right to Bald River Falls. At 14.8 miles, pass the junction with CNF Road 345, which goes left to Indian Boundary Lake. At 19 miles, park at Lake View Overlook. Since this is a one-way ride, you will need to leave a vehicle 15.5 miles farther along the Skyway, which becomes NC 143 after crossing the state line. If you are approaching the ride from the North Carolina side, Spirit Ridge is 8.6 miles west from the junction with NC 1127.

The Cherohala Skyway follows TN 165 and NC 143 across some of the wildest and most lonesome country in the Southern Appalachians. The Skyway is a spectacular scenic road, rivaled only by parts of the Blue Ridge Parkway for high elevation, scenery, and easy access to the mountains. The entire Skyway stretches 43 miles from Tellico Plains, Tennessee, to NC 1127 near Santeetlah Lake. The 4,000 feet of climbing and 40 plus miles of hills make the entire Skyway too much of a good thing for most riders, so we've selected a ride across the heart of the Skyway that lets you do most of the climbing in the car but still takes in the best of the overlooks.

Riding conditions on the Skyway are much like those on the Blue Ridge Parkway. Traffic is very light, and at least in North Carolina, the posted speed limit is 45 mph. Though there is no real shoulder on the road, drivers seem aware of cyclists, and the road has few blind spots.

After riding this spectacular route, you'll probably be a little curious about the road's history. After all, bicyclists and motor-cyclists out enjoying the scenery outnumber any cars on the road. Even the autos are mostly filled with tourists; Robbinsville to Tellico Plains has never been an important commercial route.

In fact, the idea for the Skyway began as much as a joke as anything else. In 1958 local businessmen in Tellico Plains were discussing the lack of good roads in the local mountains, perhaps with an eye on the Blue Ridge Parkway. Because they joked their roads were fit only for wagons, they sponsored wagon rides to get publicity for the idea. Their public relations campaign must have worked for by the mid-1970s construction began, but the road had also become the center of a regional controversy.

Opposition to the road came from those who recognized the Skyway's impact on the land around it. The Skyway bisects a rich, ecologically productive forest. To the north is the combined Joyce Kilmer–Slickrock Creek Wilderness in North Carolina and Citico Creek Wilderness in Tennessee, which form the second-largest wilderness area in the Southern Appalachians. To the south are the equally rugged Brushy Ridge Primitive Area and Snowbird Creek watershed. In addition to splitting this block of wild land, construction of the road caused the acidification of creeks draining from Sassafras Ridge. Much of the rock needing to be removed for the road contained sulfide minerals, which reacted with water to form weak acids. The problem halted construction for a while, but the Skyway was completed in 1996. The overall cost of the road to taxpayers was $100 million.

0.0 From Lake View Overlook (3,360 feet), turn left and ride east on the Cherohala Skyway.
Before leaving, enjoy a view north across the Cherokee National Forest to Tellico Lake on the Little Tennessee River.

0.6 Pass Eagle Gap Trailhead (3,600 feet) on the left and descend.
From Eagle Gap, Flats Mountain Trail (CNF Trail 102) leads 6.2 miles along the boundary of Citico Creek Wilderness to CNF Road 35.

1.1 Pass the unmarked start of Hemlock Creek Trail (CNF Trail 101) on the right.

2.0 After a short steep descent, reach a side road leading left to Grassy Branch Trailhead (3,400 feet).
Grassy Branch Trail (CNF Trail 91) leads 2.3 miles into Citico Creek Wilderness. A bit farther on the right is the start of McNabb Creek Trail (CNF Trail 92) leading south.

2.9 Pass Brushy Ridge Overlook on the right and ride downhill.
The views here extend south along Brushy Ridge and McIntyre Lead down to the headwaters of the Tellico River. An interpretive display at the overlook sums up philosophy of the crews who first logged these forests with the statement "They took it all."

3.9 Just beyond Charles Hall Bridge, pass a pullout for Laurel Branch Trail (CNF Trail 93) on the right.
Begin climbing.

4.1 Reach West Rattlesnake Rock Overlook (4,000 feet), a popular stop for cars and motorcycles.
This is the trailhead for Big Indian Branch Trail (CNF Trail 94) heading south and Jeffrey Hell Trail (CNF Trail 196) and Falls Branch Trail (CNF Trail 87) leading north. If you'd like to see a high mountain waterfall and are willing to gamble that

water levels are sufficient enough to make the walk worthwhile, follow Falls Branch Trail (it is the left fork after leaving the parking area) for 1.3 mostly easy miles to the falls.

4.4 Reach East Rattlesnake Rock Overlook (4,110 feet) and begin a steep climb.

Here a display tells how black bears serve as an indicator of forest health and how important the 28,000-acre Tellico Bear Preserve is to the bruin population's long-term health. If you're riding uphill in midsummer, you'll be going slow enough to spot the bright red blooms of bee balm and the orange blossoms of Turk's cap lily growing alongside the road.

5.6 Reach the North Carolina state line at Beech Gap (4,490 feet).

The gated road on the left is now part of Cold Springs Gap Trail (CNF Trail 95) leading toward Bobs Bald.

5.8 Pass Unicoi Crest Overlook.

Beech Gap marks the point where the Cherohala Skyway crosses the Tennessee–North Carolina state line.

6.3 Pass a pullout on the left at No Name Gap (4,324 feet).

7.4 Pass the intersection with Nantahala National Forest (NNF) Road 81 to Stratton Meadow.
NNF Road 81 splits off right to trailheads at Wolf Laurel and eventually joins NC 1127 close to the end of the Skyway. To the left, the road leads to the North River Road and eventually the Tellico River.

7.6 Reach Stratton Picnic Area.
There is a rest room here and a large covered signboard, handy for hiding from short summer showers.

9.2 Pass the Mud Gap Trailhead (4,480 feet).

9.5 Pass Whigg Cove Picnic Area.
Begin the long climb to the Skyway Crest.

10.6 Reach Haw Knob Overlook (4,890 feet).
The views along the long, sweeping curve of road ahead are some of the Skyway's finest.

11.8 Pass Big Junction Overlook (5,235 feet).

12.6 Reach Santeetlah Overlook Picnic Area.
At 5,390 feet it lies at the crest of the Skyway.

13.3 A paved road leads right to the picnic area and trailhead at Hooper Bald.
If the weather is good, don't miss the chance to walk the 0.5-mile round trip up to the open bald. Be aware that the Nantahala National Forest does not maintain the bald, and every year the open area gets smaller as more trees and shrubs invade the bald.

14.3 Pass the Huckleberry Trailhead on the left and begin a steep descent.

15.3 Reach the end of the ride at the Spirit Ridge Trailhead and Picnic Area.
Cap off your day with the 0.3-mile hike out to an overlook with a view of the eastern end of the Skyway. The view down toward Santeetlah Lake may make you reconsider any plans to ride to the Skyway's end.

Short and Sweet: Starting your ride at Beech Gap saves 1,000 feet of climbing but still includes most of the best views over 9.7 miles.

For Extra Credit: Starting your ride closer to Tellico Plains at Osterneck near the junction with CNF Road 210 adds over 2,000 more feet of climbing on the 29-mile, one-way ride. For the super fit, the Smoky Mountain Wheelmen also sponsors the 115-mile Cherohala Challenge that finishes on the Skyway.

6

Jake Best–Doublecamp

- **DISTANCE:** A 19-mile loop. The Short and Sweet version is a 3.4-mile loop. The Extra Credit ride from Indian Boundary Lake is 30.4 miles round trip.

- **TERRAIN:** The entire loop is on gravel and dirt forest service roads. There is a 1,700-foot climb to Salt Spring Mountain from Citico Creek.

- **SPECIAL FEATURES:** Rides along Doublecamp, Jake Best, and Citico Creeks, and a climb to an abandoned fire tower site on Salt Spring Mountain.

- **GENERAL LOCATION:** 18 miles east of Tellico Plains, Tennessee.

- **MAPS:** Trails Illustrated Tellico and Ocoee Rivers, Cherokee National Forest, TN #781.

- **ACCESS:** From the junction of TN 68 and 165 in Tellico Plains, turn east and drive 14.8 miles on TN 165 (which is also part of the Cherohala Skyway) to Cherokee National Forest (CNF) Road 345, which is usually signed for the INDIAN BOUNDARY RECREATION AREA. Turn left on CNF Road 345 and drive 1.2 miles to the junction with CNF Road 35. Bear right on gravel CNF Road 35 and drive 4.1 miles to the junction with CNF Road 59 at a designated camping area. In midsummer the camping area may resemble a refugee camp. You may want to park 2.6 miles farther down the road at the unsigned junction with CNF Road 26.

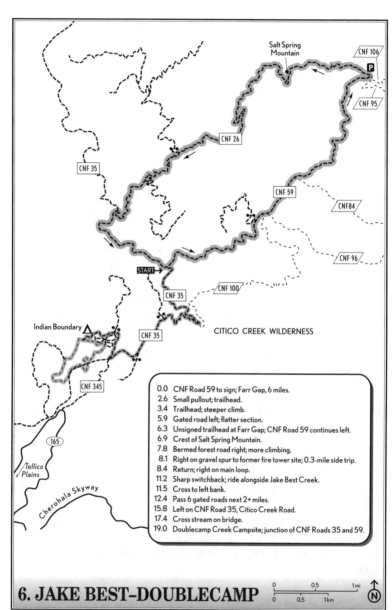

Salt Spring Mountain

CNF 106

CNF 95

CNF 26

CNF 35

CNF 59

CNF84

CNF 96

START

CNF 100

CNF 35

Indian Boundary

CNF 35

CITICO CREEK WILDERNESS

CNF 345

165

Tellico Plains

Cherohala Skyway

0.0   CNF Road 59 to sign; Farr Gap, 6 miles.
2.6   Small pullout; trailhead.
3.4   Trailhead; steeper climb.
5.9   Gated road left; flatter section.
6.3   Unsigned trailhead at Farr Gap; CNF Road 59 continues left.
6.9   Crest of Salt Spring Mountain.
7.8   Bermed forest road right; more climbing.
8.1   Right on gravel spur to former fire tower site; 0.3-mile side trip.
8.4   Return; right on main loop.
11.2 Sharp switchback; ride alongside Jake Best Creek.
11.5 Cross to left bank.
12.4 Pass 6 gated roads next 2+ miles.
15.8 Left on CNF Road 35, Citico Creek Road.
17.4 Cross stream on bridge.
19.0 Doublecamp Creek Campsite; junction of CNF Roads 35 and 59.

6. JAKE BEST–DOUBLECAMP

0   0.5   1mi
0   0.5   1km

N

Doublecamp and Jake Best Creeks are wedged between two of the prime recreation areas in the southern half of the Cherokee National Forest. To the west is the heavily used Citico Creek corridor along CNF Road 35. Here visitors are drawn by pleasant, but often crowded, camping, easily accessible swimming holes, and fine fishing. Camping along the Citico Creek corridor is restricted to designated roadside areas, which are first-come, first-served sites. To the east is the less-traveled Citico Creek Wilderness, where a network of rugged and seldom-trod trails leads from the headwaters of Citico Creek to the crest of the Unicoi Mountains. Of all the rides described in this guide, Jake Best-Doublecamp is the farthest from any town.

Jake Best-Doublecamp links primitive forest service roads along the two creeks with the well-traveled gravel road along Citico Creek. The loop circles Cowcamp Ridge, a remote area where the only access is via long closed forest roads. Cowcamp Ridge is not wilderness but part of the Cherokee National Forest's Tellico Bear Preserve, where bear hunting is not allowed.

The ride is essentially one long climb from CNF Road 35 past Farr Gap to the old fire tower site on Salt Spring Mountain. The tower, like most on forest service and state lands in Tennessee, has been removed, but the site is still a high, cool spot to rest after the long climb.

Though the loop is easy to follow, don't expect a lot of signs along the way. In general the roads and trails in Cherokee National Forest are poorly signed, even in comparison to other national forests, and few of the paved road intersections with TN 165 and the Cherohala Skyway are signed.

0.0 Ride up CNF Road 59 where a sign indicates that Farr Gap is 6 miles away.
CNF Road 59 is a well-maintained dirt road that follows a gentle route along the left bank of Doublecamp Creek. Watch for waterfalls, cascades, swimming holes, and fishing spots in this cool, clear water.

2.4 Gated CNF Road 402301 is on the left.
The road soon reaches two campsites and crosses to the right bank at the north trailhead for Rocky Flats Trail (CNF Trail 100).

2.6 A small pullout marks the trailhead for Mill Branch Trail (CNF Trail 96).

3.4 Reach the trailhead for Crowder Branch Trail (CNF Trail 84).
There is a small pullout just before the road crosses to the left bank of Doublecamp Creek. A closed road leads north by the bridge. From this point, the road pulls away from the creek and begins to climb more steeply toward Farr Gap.

5.9 A gated road on the left marks the start of a flatter section that passes a small campsite.

6.3 Reach the unsigned trailhead at Farr Gap.
There is parking for several vehicles and room for horse trailers, though there is no sign of horses using the area. To the right Stiffknee (CNF Trail 106) and Fodderstack (CNF Trail 95) Trails begin down a blocked old road. An even older road can still be found diving off the north slope of the gap. CNF Road 59 continues to the left from the trailhead.

6.9 Reach the end of the climb at the crest of Salt Spring Mountain.

7.8 Pass a bermed forest road on the right and begin to climb again.

8.1 Turn right on the gravel spur road to the former fire tower site.
The fire tower site is a 0.3-mile side trip. Though the tower is gone and trees have grown up to obscure the view, the site is still a cool breezy refuge from the heat for tired summer riders. It's also a great spot to rest up for the long downhill ride to come.

8.4 Return to main loop and turn right.
At some point CNF Road 59 has been renamed CNF Road 26. Begin a long fast descent on a generally well-maintained dirt road. Along the upper slopes are views of Cowcamp Ridge, which you are circling around. The ridge is part of the Tellico Bear Preserve. Much of the forest slope here is thick stands of pine that have been killed by the Southern pine beetle. Be alert for downed trees along the road.

11.2 After turning a sharp switchback pull alongside Jake Best Creek.
The grade along the creek is much gentler.

11.5 Cross to the left bank of the creek.

12.4 Pass a gated road on the left beside a small creek.

13.0 Pass the gated and signed gravel CNF Road 5022 on the right.
Start a rolling section of trail.

Citico Creek near the confluence with Jake Best Creek

14.0 Pass a gated dirt road on the right.

14.3 Pass gated CNF Road 2604 on the left.
Begin a fast downhill.

14.6 Pass a gated road on the right.

14.8 Pass a gated road on the left and a small campsite on the right.

15.8 Turn left on CNF Road 35, Citico Creek Road.
For the next 3 miles, CNF Road 35 hugs the banks of Citico Creek, a lovely stream, fruitful fishing destination, and popular camping area. This road is heavily used, so be sure to watch for traffic.

17.4 Cross a side stream on a short bridge.

19.0 Reach Doublecamp Creek Campsite and the junction of CNF Roads 35 and 59.

Short and Sweet: Since there is no way to cut this loop short, consider riding the gentle and scenic 3.4-mile loop trail around Indian Boundary Lake if you are looking for an alternative to this ride. The easiest place to access the trail is from the parking area by the swimming area. Though no signs mark the trail, it is easy to find the gravel path between the parking area and beach. Indian Boundary is a fee area, but a cool swim after a hot ride is well worth the $2 (in 2002) price.

For Extra Credit: Starting your ride at Indian Boundary Lake makes the ride 30.4 miles round trip and adds a 400-foot climb back to the lake.

IN AND
AROUND
THE SMOKIES

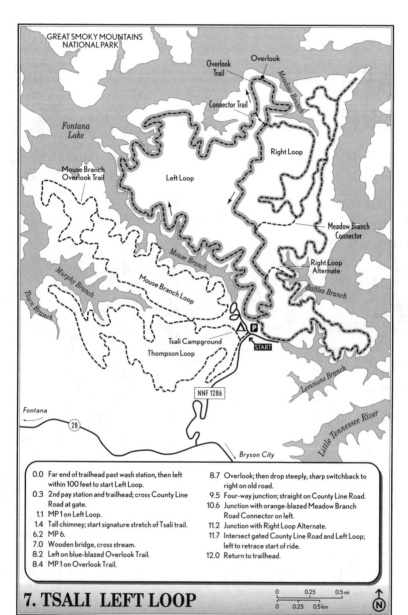

GREAT SMOKY MOUNTAINS
NATIONAL PARK

Overlook
Overlook
Trail

Connector Trail

Fontana
Lake

Right Loop

Mouse Branch
Overlook Trail

Left Loop

Meadow Branch
Connector

Mouse Branch

Right Loop
Alternate

Murphy Branch

Mouse Branch Loop

Battles Branch

Town Branch

Tsali Campground

Thompson Loop

START

Lemmons Branch

NNF 1286

Fontana

28

Bryson City

Little Tennessee River

0.0 Far end of trailhead past wash station, then left
     within 100 feet to start Left Loop.
0.3 2nd pay station and trailhead; cross County Line
     Road at gate.
1.1 MP 1 on Left Loop.
1.4 Tall chimney; start signature stretch of Tsali trail.
6.2 MP 6.
7.0 Wooden bridge, cross stream.
8.2 Left on blue-blazed Overlook Trail.
8.4 MP 1 on Overlook Trail.

8.7 Overlook; then drop steeply, sharp switchback to
     right on old road.
9.5 Four-way junction; straight on County Line Road.
10.6 Junction with orange-blazed Meadow Branch
     Road Connector on left.
11.2 Junction with Right Loop Alternate.
11.7 Intersect gated County Line Road and Left Loop;
     left to retrace start of ride.
12.0 Return to trailhead.

7. TSALI LEFT LOOP

0   0.25   0.5 mi
0   0.25   0.5 km

N

Tsali Left Loop

- **DISTANCE:** 12 miles around Left Loop and Overlook Trail. The Short and Sweet version is an 7.7-mile loop around part of Right Loop. The Extra Credit ride is 18.2 miles around Left Loop and Right Loop.

- **TERRAIN:** Mostly rolling singletrack with some technical difficulty, plus a return on an old road in the Cheoah Ranger District of the Nantahala National Forest.

- **SPECIAL FEATURES:** The ride hugs the shore of Fontana Lake and has some of the most exhilarating singletrack in the Southeast.

- **GENERAL LOCATION:** About 20 miles west of Cherokee, North Carolina.

- **MAPS:** Tsali Recreation Area pamphlet is available from the Cheoah Ranger District.

- **ACCESS:** To reach Tsali Recreation Area, drive 8.1 miles east on NC 28 from the junction of NC 143 and 28, or 2.9 miles west on NC 28 from the junction of NC 28 and US 19/74. Look for the TSALI RECREATION AREA sign at the start of paved National Nantahala Forest Road (NNF) 1286. Drive 1.5 miles to a four-way junction where the trailhead is straight ahead, the campground is to the left, and access to a boat ramp is to the right. For day use, park at the trailhead and pay the $2 per person fee.

Almost since the first pair of knobbies hit the dirt, Tsali has been the place that all mountain biking trails in the region have been measured against. And the legend continues to grow of scenic stretches of shoreline singletrack, long smooth downhills, and short gentle climbs. Tsali is an area that lives up to its hype and delivers even more.

Four loops radiate away from the campground at the heart of Tsali Recreation Area. To avoid user conflicts, two loops are open every day to mountain bikers, and the other two are open to horseback riders. Hikers can use any trail any day. As of 2003, Mouse Branch and Thompson Loops are open Tuesday, Thursday, and Saturday to mountain bikers, and Right and Left Loops are open Monday, Wednesday, Friday, and Sunday to mountain bikers. In practice, few hikers, and even fewer horseback riders, use the area.

Tsali Campground is the perfect base for exploring the trails, which begin nearly out the door of your tent. There are 42 sites, plus flush toilets and hot showers in the summer season for $15. During the off-season, the water is shut off and the fee drops to $5. The trailhead has room for more than 50 vehicles, a sign board is well stocked with trail maps, and there is a handy bike wash station. The Nantahala National Forest staffs the trailhead in summer. A concession stand offering snacks, cold drinks, souvenirs, and some biking supplies also operates seasonally.

So what is it exactly that makes this area so popular? Riders used to the big mountains and wide open spaces of Western landscapes might scoff at gentler trails around a wooded lakeshore, but Tsali offers some features rarely found in this region. The trails are nearly all singletrack, much of them built with mountain bikers in mind. The lakeside trail sections are remarkably pretty. Fontana has escaped much of the development that plagues other Tennessee Valley Authority (TVA) lakes. Other mountain bike trails resemble green tunnels in summer; few have as many vistas as Tsali. There are long gradual downhills where the twists and turns make you feel like a downhill skier carving turns. The trails here are usually hard-packed dirt, with some rougher spots on hills or where small streams are crossed. And, the climbs are generally short and rideable for most cyclists. All in all, this adds up to an area where the average rider can enjoy the adrenaline rush of fast, winding, and rolling trails with scenery unsurpassed by other mountain biking areas.

0.0 Begin your ride at the far end of the trailhead.
Ride past the bike wash station and then look for a sharp left turn within 100 feet that marks the start of Left Loop. The trail is easy to follow and is sporadically marked with blue-and-green-paint blazes. As with all Tsali trails, the trail junctions are well marked.

0.3 Reach a second pay station and trailhead where the trail crosses County Line Road at a gate.

1.1 Reach milepost 1 on Left Loop.
All the trails at Tsali are marked with these posts, which generally are found at 0.5-mile intervals. Here the trail lies just above the usually dry arm of Mouse Branch.

1.4 Pass a tall chimney that is the only reminder of an old home site.
Fontana Dam was constructed near the end of World War II to provide power for the TVA. The dam, the highest in the eastern United States, flooded some of the richest farmland in the Southern Appalachians and isolated some small towns and family farms. This home site may have been abandoned because of the construction of the dam.

You will next begin the signature stretch of Tsali trail. Left Loop winds close by the lakeshore, offering many views across Mouse Branch to a ridge, traversed by Mouse Branch Loop, and later across Fontana Lake to parts of Great Smoky Mountains National Park. The trail is tight and twisty, the tread is smooth, except where it crosses small drainages, and none of the hills along the way is too long or too steep. The riding is ideal.

6.2 Reach milepost 6.
Here the trail becomes hillier, and the riding becomes more difficult. You'll climb up and over two small knobs and then begin the climb to the junction with Overlook Trail.

7.0 The trail uses a narrow wooden bridge to cross a small stream.

8.2 Reach the signed junction with Overlook Trail.
To the right, County Line Road leads 2.6 miles back to the trailhead. If you elect to skip the overlook, this will cut your ride short by 1.1 miles. Turn left to ride Overlook Trail, which has blue blazes.

8.4 Reach milepost 1 on Overlook Trail.
The mileposts on Overlook Trail are numbered for riders coming from Right Loop.

8.7 Reach the overlook.
This is a great place to relax in the shade and enjoy the views across Fontana Lake to Great Smoky Mountains National Park. The large bay straight across from the overlook is where the Tuckasegee River joins the Little Tennessee River. You'll also notice that many of the pine trees at the overlook are dead. The have been killed by the Southern pine beetle, a small insect that feeds on the trees' inner core.

Beyond the overlook, the trail drops steeply and makes a sharp switchback to the right on an old road.

9.5 Reach a signed four-way junction.
To the right is the 0.1-mile connector leading back to the start of Overlook Trail. To the left is Right Loop, which leads 8 miles back to the trailhead. Go straight and uphill to follow County Line Road back to the trailhead. County Line Road is a wide, well-maintained road that will pass two old logging roads and a wildlife opening leading west.

10.6 Reach the junction with the orange-blazed Meadow Branch Road Connector on the left.
This old road leads about 0.5-mile east to join Right Loop near milepost 6.

11.2 Reach the junction with Right Loop Alternate Trail.
This singletrack connector leads east to Right Loop near milepost 3.5.

11.7 Reach the intersection of County Line Road and Left Loop at the gate across County Line Road. Turn left here to retrace the start of your ride back to the trailhead.
Alternatively, you can stay on County Line Road to reach the four-way junction at the end of the paved NNF Road 1286 in 0.2 mile.

12.0 Return to the trailhead at Tsali.

Short and Sweet: Use Meadow Branch Road Connector to leave Right Loop at milepost 6 and make a 7.7-mile loop by returning on County Line Road.

For Extra Credit: If you ride Left and Right Loops together, you will cover 18.2 miles.

8

Tsali Mouse Branch Loop

- **DISTANCE:** A 10.2-mile loop. The Short and Sweet version is a 7.3-mile loop. The Extra Credit Ride is a 16.3-mile loop.

- **TERRAIN:** Moderate singletrack and two-track mountain biking trails over rolling terrain with some technical difficulty in the Cheoah Ranger District of the Nantahala National Forest.

- **SPECIAL FEATURES:** The easiest loop at Tsali has a great overlook above Fontana Lake.

- **GENERAL LOCATION:** About 20 miles west of Cherokee, North Carolina.

- **MAPS:** Tsali Recreation Area pamphlet is available from the Cheoah Ranger District.

- **ACCESS:** To reach Tsali Recreation Area, drive 8.1 miles east on NC 28 from the junction of NC 143 and NC 28, or 2.9 miles west on NC 28 from the junction of NC 28 and US 19/74. Look for the TSALI RECREATION AREA sign at the start of the paved Nantahala National Forest Road (NNF) 1286. Drive 1.5 miles to a four-way junction where the trailhead is straight ahead, the campground is to the left and access to a boat ramp is to the right. For day use, park at the trailhead and pay the $2 per person fee.

If you arrive at Tsali on a Saturday, Tuesday, or Thursday, your riding choices are Mouse Branch and Thompson Loops. Like the neighboring Left and Right Loops, Mouse Branch and Thompson Loops are a mix of singletrack trail and two-track old roads. Of the

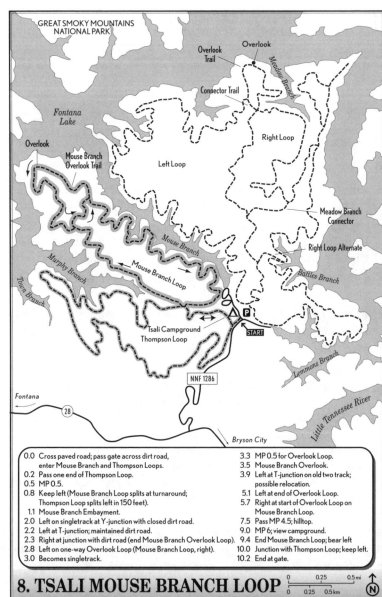

GREAT SMOKY MOUNTAINS
NATIONAL PARK

Overlook
Trail
Overlook

Meadow Branch

Connector Trail

*Fontana
Lake*

Right Loop

Overlook

Mouse Branch
Overlook Trail

Left Loop

Meadow Branch
Connector

Mouse Branch

Right Loop Alternate

Murphy Branch

Mouse Branch
Loop

Mouse Branch Loop

Battles Branch

Town Branch

Tsali Campground
Thompson Loop

P

START

Lemmons Branch

NNF 1286

Fontana

28

Bryson City

Little Tennessee River

0.0	Cross paved road; pass gate across dirt road, enter Mouse Branch and Thompson Loops.
0.2	Pass one end of Thompson Loop.
0.5	MP 0.5.
0.8	Keep left (Mouse Branch Loop splits at turnaround; Thompson Loop splits left in 150 feet).
1.1	Mouse Branch Embayment.
2.0	Left on singletrack at Y-junction with closed dirt road.
2.2	Left at T-junction; maintained dirt road.
2.3	Right at junction with dirt road (end Mouse Branch Overlook Loop).
2.8	Left on one-way Overlook Loop (Mouse Branch Loop, right).
3.0	Becomes singletrack.

3.3	MP 0.5 for Overlook Loop.
3.5	Mouse Branch Overlook.
3.9	Left at T-junction on old two track; possible relocation.
5.1	Left at end of Overlook Loop.
5.7	Right at start of Overlook Loop on Mouse Branch Loop.
7.5	Pass MP 4.5; hilltop.
9.0	MP 6; view campground.
9.4	End Mouse Branch Loop; bear left
10.0	Junction with Thompson Loop; keep left.
10.2	End at gate.

8. TSALI MOUSE BRANCH LOOP

0   0.25   0.5 mi
0   0.25   0.5 km

N

four loop trails at Tsali, Mouse Branch is generally considered the easiest; and Thompson, the hardest. According to the Nantahala National Forest trailhead hosts, Mouse Branch Loop has been ridden on a mountain unicycle. But it's not that easy. There are enough hills, narrow tread, and muddy potholes to scare off riders with no trail experience. Since the trailhead hosts have seen more than their share of mountain bikers heading off into the woods, we'll take their word for it and imagine there's a unicycle rider out there of unimaginable skill. Mouse Branch Loop is rideable for those with little singletrack experience and fun enough for riders with thousands of miles on their odometers.

Like all the Tsali trails, Mouse Branch Loop was built with mountain bikers in mind. The loop is well marked and easy to follow, and you can track your progress by the posts spaced at 0.5-mile intervals. Though open to horseback riders four days a week, the trail shows little sign of horse use. If you ride the loops in their recommended direction (following the mileposts) you'll see relatively few other riders on these popular trails.

The highlight of the ride is the overlook high above Fontana Lake. Just across the lake is one of the wildest parts of Great Smoky Mountains National Park. Mountain biking in the Smokies is allowed only on three short trails, which follow old roads, so riding at Tsali is as close as you can get to a fat tire trip through the park.

For more background on Tsali, see Tsali Left Loop (ride #7).

0.0 From the trailhead, ride across the paved road and past a gate across a dirt road that marks the entry to Mouse Branch and Thompson Loops.
Your route will be a figure eight that begins on Mouse Branch Loop and includes the Mouse Branch Overlook Loop.

0.2 Pass one end of Thompson Loop, which intersects from the left near a stream crossing.

0.5 Pass milepost 0.5.
The Tsali trails are all marked by posts at 0.5-mile intervals.

0.8 Keep left where Mouse Branch Loop splits off at a turnaround in the road.
Just 150 feet farther, Thompson Loop splits off to the left.

1.1 The trail narrows and begins to roll and twist along the shore of the Mouse Branch Embayment of Fontana Lake.
The embayment will be dry in the upper reaches when lake levels are low.

2.0 Turn left on a singletrack at a Y-junction with a closed dirt road.
Just beyond, begin a short climb near milepost 2.

2.2 Turn left at a T-junction with a maintained dirt road.

2.3 Go right at a junction with a dirt road that is the end of Mouse Branch Overlook Loop.
You will make a short climb to the crest of the ridge that divides Mouse and Murphy Branches.

2.8 Turn left on the one-way Mouse Branch Overlook Loop where Mouse Branch Loop turns right.

3.0 The trail becomes singletrack.

3.3 Reach milepost 0.5 on Mouse Branch Overlook Loop.

3.5 Arrive at Mouse Branch Overlook.
Directly below are the cool, clear waters of Fontana Lake. Across the lake is the rugged and empty terrain around Welch Ridge in Great Smoky Mountains National Park. A marina just west of Tsali provides access to a small community of houseboats anchored along the lakeshore. Be careful around the overlook when the wind is up. Most of the pine trees have been killed by the Southern pine beetle.

3.9 Turn left at a T-junction on an old two-track road.
By the time this book is published, the Cheoah Ranger District will have completed a relocation of the trail off this old road.

5.1 Turn left at the end of Overlook Loop to retrace your climb up the divide between Mouse and Murphy Branches.

5.7 This time, turn right at the start of Mouse Branch Overlook Loop on Mouse Branch Loop to return to the trailhead.
The trail here is a downhill singletrack carved into a very steep slope.

7.5 Pass milepost 4.5 on a hilltop after making a short climb.

9.0 Reach milepost 6 and a view of the campground just beyond.

Mouse Branch Overlook extends over Fontana Dam to Great Smoky Mountains Natonal Park

9.4 Bear left at the end of Mouse Branch Loop and retrace your route to Tsali Trailhead.

10.0 Keep left again at the junction with Thompson Loop.

10.2 End your ride at the gate across the paved road from the trailhead at Tsali.

Short and Sweet: If you skip Mouse Branch Overlook Loop, your ride will be 7.3 miles.

For Extra Credit: You can add Thompson Loop for a 16.3-mile ride. Of the four Tsali loops, Thompson is considered the most difficult. The loop is a bit more technical than the other loops and has a few more mud holes.

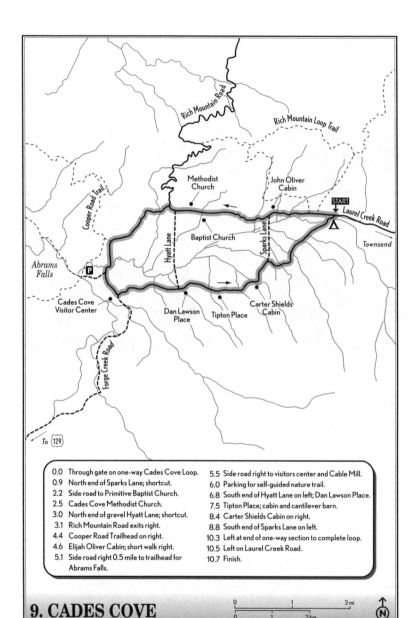

Rich Mountain Road

Rich Mountain Loop Trail

Cooper Road Trail

Methodist Church

John Oliver Cabin

START

Laurel Creek Road

Townsend

Baptist Church

Hyatt Lane

Sparks Lane

Abrams Falls

P

Cades Cove Visitor Center

Dan Lawson Place

Tipton Place

Carter Shields Cabin

Forge Creek Road

To 129

0.0 Through gate on one-way Cades Cove Loop.
0.9 North end of Sparks Lane; shortcut.
2.2 Side road to Primitive Baptist Church.
2.5 Cades Cove Methodist Church.
3.0 North end of gravel Hyatt Lane; shortcut.
3.1 Rich Mountain Road exits right.
4.4 Cooper Road Trailhead on right.
4.6 Elijah Oliver Cabin; short walk right.
5.1 Side road right 0.5 mile to trailhead for Abrams Falls.

5.5 Side road right to visitors center and Cable Mill.
6.0 Parking for self-guided nature trail.
6.8 South end of Hyatt Lane on left; Dan Lawson Place.
7.5 Tipton Place; cabin and cantilever barn.
8.4 Carter Shields Cabin on right.
8.8 South end of Sparks Lane on left.
10.3 Left at end of one-way section to complete loop.
10.5 Left on Laurel Creek Road.
10.7 Finish.

9. CADES COVE

0   1   2 mi
0   1   2 km

N

Cades Cove

- **DISTANCE:** A 10.7-mile loop. The Short and Sweet version is a 3.7-mile loop. The Extra Credit ride is 31.3 miles, including a side trip.

- **TERRAIN:** The loop follows a busy and narrow one-way paved road through Great Smoky Mountains National Park.

- **SPECIAL FEATURES:** Wildlife watching and visits to pioneer homesteads.

- **GENERAL LOCATION:** About 10 miles southwest of Townsend, Tennessee.

- **MAPS:** Great Smoky Mountains National Park Official Map and Guide is available at many locations around the park.

- **ACCESS:** From the intersection of US 321 and TN 73 in Townsend, drive south on TN 73 into the park. In 2.2 miles, reach the intersection called the Townsend Y, and turn right on Laurel Creek Road. At 9.9 miles, reach Cades Cove and the start of the loop road. Continue straight for 0.1 mile to the large parking area immediately before the gate at the start of the one-way portion of Cades Cove Loop. Be sure to pick up a copy of the Cades Cove Tour brochure at the Orientation Shelter near the parking area.

Cades Cove is the signature feature of America's most visited national park. As such, the winding, narrow road through it can be crowded, sometimes insanely so. With about 2 million visitors a year, it receives more guests than 90 percent of other national parks. The Park Service advises drivers to plan on up to four hours to complete the 11-mile loop at popular times, such as summer weekends and during the fall color season. But the Park Service also recognizes the recreational value of the road and closes it to vehicles on Wednesdays and Saturdays until 10AM during the summer from early May until late September. The loop road is also closed to vehicles from sunset until dawn. Due to the heavy traffic and high percentage of distracted drivers, it is safest to ride the loop during the Wednesday and Saturday closures or very early in the morning on other days when traffic is light.

Cades Cove is also a good example of the often conflicting

One of the many historic barns preserved in Cades Cove

missions of the Park Service. The Cove is one of the Smokies' most historic areas. A number of pre-park homesteads, early churches, and a water-powered mill are preserved here to offer visitors a glimpse of pre-park life. But the Cove is also a good example of the Smokies' mission to preserve, and often restore, the complex natural habitats protected in national parks.

For many years the fields in Cades Cove were leased for harvesting hay and livestock grazing. Kermit Caughron, the last of the Cove's original residents allowed to live there under a special-use permit, raised cattle here until his death in 1999. Beginning in 1996, the park began a new management plan for 3,000 acres of open grasslands that included the elimination of the hay and grazing leases because of their adverse impacts on wildlife and water quality. The park's goal is to enrich both natural and cultural resources throughout Cades Cove. Aerial photographs taken in 1946 show that the Cove then was a patchwork of small fields. Settlers typically had only a dozen or so cows, which they grazed on hillsides, balds, or woodlots, the valley bottom being too valuable as cropland to allow grazing.

New techniques to manage Cades Cove include prescribed burns, restoring native plants, and annual mowing. Nonnative grasses like fescue, introduced in the later hay and grazing operations, are being replaced with native grasses that provide better food and shelter for wildlife and increase native plant diversity.

Wildlife is Cades Cove's biggest attraction. Though the grasslands provide some of the best views of the Smoky Mountains from anywhere in east Tennessee, it is deer and black bear that most people come to see. If you ride the loop road at dusk or dawn, you're almost guaranteed to see a few bucks or does, feeding nearby. More rare, but still seen, are black bear, wild turkey, and other game. It is the practice of stopping in the middle of the road to watch or photograph wildlife that leads to the "deer jams" and "bear jams," which make navigating the loop by car so slow.

Despite the crowds, Cades Cove Loop remains a popular ride with family groups and experienced cyclists alike. Due to previous bicycling accidents, there are two downhill sections along the loop where park officials ask bicyclists to walk their bikes. With public input, the Park Service is also in the process of revising their management plan for Cades Cove, which may include adopting some sort of public transportation to reduce traffic congestion. Check the park's web site for more information about this issue.

0.0 Ride through the gate on the one-way portion of Cades Cove Loop.
The road is narrow and winding. Be careful to watch the road and be aware of vehicles around you.

0.9 Reach the north end of Sparks Lane, one of two gravel roads that bisects Cades Cove.
This shortcut will lead 2.8 miles back to the parking area. Just beyond the intersection is the John Oliver Cabin. This log home, with its stacked stone chimney and spacious porches, was built in the 1820s and is the oldest home remaining in Cades Cove.

2.2 A side road leads left 0.3 mile to the Primitive Baptist Church.

2.5 Cades Cove Methodist Church was built in 1902.

3.0 Reach the north end of the gravel Hyatt Lane.
This shortcut will lead 5.3 miles back to the parking area.

3.1 Rich Mountain Road exits to the right.
This one-way gravel road climbs to the park boundary in 6.8 miles. It then descends into Tuckaleechee Cove near Townsend. The road is closed in winter to vehicles, but bicycles and pedestrians are welcome year-round.

4.4 Pass the Cooper Road Trailhead on the right.
Before the establishment of the national park, this was the primary road between Cades Cove and Maryville, Tennessee. Now it is an important hiking trail.

4.6 The Elijah Oliver Cabin is a short walk to the right.
Elijah Oliver built this cabin when he moved back to Cades Cove after the Civil War.

5.1 A side road leads right 0.5 mile to the trailhead for the popular 5-mile round-trip walk to Abrams Falls.

5.5 A side road leads right to Cades Cove Visitor Center and Cable Mill.
Here you can browse the displays at the visitor center, learn how an 1870s-era sawmill worked, and explore the outbuildings of a 19th-century farm. There are

rest rooms at the visitor center. The gravel Forge Creek Road also enters here. You can exit Cades Cove to US 129 via Forge Creek and the one-way Parson Branch Road in 10 miles.

6.0 Pass the parking area for Cades Cove Self-Guiding Nature Trail.
This 0.5-mile loop illustrates the many ways early settlers used the variety of tree species present in Cades Cove.

6.8 The south end of Hyatt Lane enters on the left.
Immediately beyond is the Dan Lawson Place. This unusual cabin was originally built from logs, but later additions used sawed lumber.

7.5 Pass the Tipton Place with its cabin and handsome cantilever barn.

8.4 Pass the Carter Shields Cabin on the right.

8.8 The south end of Sparks Lane enters on the left.

10.3 Turn left at the end of the one-way section to complete the loop road.
The road to the right leads to Cades Cove Campground, a ranger station, and a small campground store. Cades Cove Campground is open year-round, accepts reservations from May 15th to October 31st, and has 161 sites. The road to the left will lead past the entrance stable for the horseback-riding concession. Next pass a road leading right to Cades Cove Picnic Area.

10.5 Turn left on Laurel Creek Road to reach the parking area.

10.7 Finish your ride.

Short and Sweet: You can make a 3.7-mile loop using 0.9-mile Sparks Lane as a shortcut. If you cut the loop short at Hyatt Lane, your ride will be 8.3 miles.

For Extra Credit: You can exit the loop on the gravel Forge Creek and Parson Branch Roads to ride 10.3 miles one way to US 129 at the park boundary. This round trip will yield a 31.3-mile ride. A mountain bike is recommended for these roads.

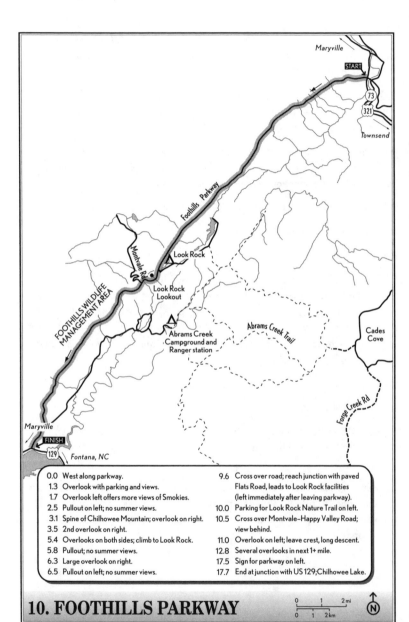

0.0 West along parkway.	9.6 Cross over road; reach junction with paved Flats Road, leads to Look Rock facilities (left immediately after leaving parkway).
1.3 Overlook with parking and views.	
1.7 Overlook left offers more views of Smokies.	
2.5 Pullout on left; no summer views.	10.0 Parking for Look Rock Nature Trail on left.
3.1 Spine of Chilhowee Mountain; overlook on right.	10.5 Cross over Montvale–Happy Valley Road; view behind.
3.5 2nd overlook on right.	11.0 Overlook on left; leave crest, long descent.
5.4 Overlooks on both sides; climb to Look Rock.	12.8 Several overlooks in next 1+ mile.
5.8 Pullout; no summer views.	17.5 Sign for parkway on left.
6.3 Large overlook on right.	17.7 End at junction with US 129; Chilhowee Lake.
6.5 Pullout on left; no summer views.	

10. FOOTHILLS PARKWAY

0   1   2 mi
0   1   2 km

N

© The Countryman Press

Foothills Parkway

- **DISTANCE:** 17.7 miles one way. The Short and Sweet version is 9.6 miles one way. The Extra Credit ride is 35.4 miles round trip.

- **TERRAIN:** This ride is on paved roads in Great Smoky Mountains National Park and includes a climb of 1,400 feet from US 321 to Look Rock.

- **SPECIAL FEATURES:** This extremely scenic ride follows a very low-traffic road. The 1-mile, round-trip hike to the tower on top of Look Rock leads to one of the very best views of the Smoky Mountains. The parkway between Look Rock and US 129 was closed in May 2003 by flood damage. The Park Service plans to have the road open by June 2004.

- **GENERAL LOCATION:** 15 miles south of Maryville, Tennessee.

- **MAPS:** Great Smoky Mountains National Park Official Map and Guide is available at many locations around the park.

- **ACCESS:** From the junction of US 321 and Washington Street on the south side of Maryville, drive south on US 321 toward Townsend. Once out of Maryville, US 321 is a designated bike route with a wide shoulder. In 15 miles, in the community of Walland, look for the signed exit for the Foothills Parkway. Turn left at the bottom of the exit road and park on the broad shoulder near, but not blocking, a gate. To leave a car at the end of the ride, drive 17.5 miles along the parkway to the junction with US 129 and leave a car at a pullout near the parkway sign.

The Foothills Parkway was first conceived as a scenic highway to parallel the Tennessee boundary of Great Smoky Mountains National Park from Chilhowee Lake (US 129) to the Pigeon River near Cosby (I-40). Legislation authorizing the 72-mile parkway was passed in 1944. Construction of the two segments now open was started in 1960 and completed in 1968. Along with the section between Walland and US 129 described here, a short stretch on the east end between I-40 and Cosby was also built at this time. Construction of a third section spanning 16.1 miles between US 321 in Walland and Wear Valley was started in 1982 and then halted in 1989, leaving an especially troublesome 1.6-mile missing link in the middle of the proposed route.

In 1999, construction was restarted on the missing link when a $12.8-million contract was let to build just 2 of the 10 bridges engineers estimated would be needed. Construction of the entire missing link is expected to cost $90 million. The Park Service is now considering using retaining walls instead of bridges to span this gap. Once this decision is reached, contracts would be awarded that will allow the 16.1 miles between Walland and Wear Valley to be opened. The unfinished portion between Walland and Wear Valley is open to hikers, cyclists, and horseback riders, except during periods of construction.

Construction costs remain the main roadblock to further extensions of the parkway. Estimates of money spent to date were as high as $65 million in 2001 dollars, with up to another $340 million needed to complete the unfinished segments between Wear Valley and Cosby. By comparison, the most recent fiscal year operating budget for the entire park was a measly $15.4 million.

Much of the land to the north of the Foothills Parkway on the US 129 end is now part of the Foothills Wildlife Management Area, which is managed by the Tennessee Wildlife Resources Agency. The establishment of the area is the result of the efforts of the Foothills Land Conservancy, a private organization that identified the land as a critical adjunct to black bear habitat around the national park and then raised the $12.5 million needed to buy the 5,800 acres. Though the parkway bisects the area, there is currently no public access from the parkway.

A $12 million pair of bridges mark the end of the closed section of the Foothills Parkway between Walland and Wear Valley

0.0 Begin by riding west along the Foothills Parkway.
The parkway is a two-lane scenic road with a maximum speed of 45 mph. It will feel very familiar to those who have ridden on the Blue Ridge Parkway. With the exception of water and rest rooms at Look Rock (in season), there are no facilities along this road. The ride begins with a vigorous climb.

1.3 An overlook with a huge parking area offers views southeast over the valley of Hesse Creek to the northeast corner of Great Smoky Mountains National Park.
The Foothills Parkway begins a long climb up the southeast face of Chilhowee Mountain.

1.7 An overlook on the left offers more views of the Great Smoky Mountains.
The crest of Chilhowee Mountain to the right of the parkway recently burned. Many dead trees from the fire still remain standing.

2.5 A pullout on the left side offers no views in summer.

3.1 Reach the spine of Chilhowee Mountain at an overlook on the right.
Begin a well-deserved downhill stretch.

3.5 Reach a second overlook on the right.

5.4 Overlooks on both sides of the parkway mark the start of the final long climb to Look Rock.
The blaze that burned on Chilhowee Mountain was near peak intensity here. Burned and downed pine trees litter the forest floor. Though some pines were killed by the blaze, others here have been killed by the Southern pine beetle, a pest that bores into the tree's living tissue, eventually killing it. The beetle's effects are even more pronounced farther north in Tennessee, where larger pine forests on the Cumberland Plateau have been devastated. The combination of insect-killed trees and dry conditions is likely to contribute to future fires along Chilhowee Mountain.

5.8 A pullout with no summer views marks the end of the burn.
The towers on the hillside to the left are part of Top of the World Estates, a development in the narrow strip of private land between the parkway and Great Smoky Mountains National Park. You will soon cross over Butterfly Gap Road leading from Top of the World Estates.

6.3 Pass a large overlook on the right.

6.5 A pullout on the left offers no summer views.

7.9 The long, steep grade to Look Rock finally begins to ease.

9.6 Just after crossing over the road to Look Rock Picnic Area, reach the junction with the paved Flats Road, which leads to Look Rock Campground, as well as the picnic area and Top of the World Estates.
Here a sign tells you that US 321 is 11 miles back and US 129 is 7 miles ahead.

To reach the Look Rock facilities, turn left immediately after leaving the parkway. At the sign-in station, the left fork leads to the picnic area, which has an open rest room during the summer season. The road straight ahead leads to the 68-unit campground, which is open from around May 15th to October 31st. There is water seasonally at the ranger station, a welcome roof if you happen to choose to ride on a rainy day or need some shade on a sunny one.

10.0 Descend to the parking area for Look Rock Nature Trail on the left.
The asphalt trail is a 1-mile, round-trip hike. The concrete tower and three-tiered ramp on top of Look Rock are similar to the far more visited tower atop the park's highpoint at Clingmans Dome. If you can't see all the way to Clingmans Dome, perhaps the problem is the park's famous haze (hence the name Smoky Mountains). However, in modern times, not all of this haze is simply the natural product of heat and humidity. The Smokies has some of the worst air quality of any national park. Between May 1998 and December 2001, the recommended 8-hour ozone limit was exceeded on 142 days. Since 1948, visibility in the park has decreased 40 percent. If you'd like to check on air quality and weather conditions before your ride, you can view current conditions at the air-quality-monitoring station near the Look Rock Tower at www.nature.nps.gov/ard/parks/grsm/lookrock-weather.htm. On clear days the view from the tower extends along the Smokies crest from Mount Guyot to the aptly named Thunderhead Mountain.

10.5 Cross over Montvale-Happy Valley Road and enjoy the view behind you to Look Rock Tower.

11.0 Reach another fine overlook on the left with views of the community of Happy Valley.
The parkway now leaves the crest of Chilhowee Mountain and begins a long descent down its south face.

12.8 The high peak visible to the southeast is Gregory Bald on the crest of the Smokies.

13.1 There is another overlook on the left next to a grove of pine trees killed by the Southern pine beetle.

13.5 Pass an overlook on the left.

14.0 Pass another overlook with views over Happy Valley.
For the last 0.5 miles of the ride, an embayment of Chilhowee Lake is on your left.

14.5 Reach the site of the May 2003 washout.
Exceptionally strong storms in May 2003 damaged a number of roads in both Great Smoky Mountains National Park and surrounding area. Here the fill material used to carry the parkway above a small unnamed stream was washed away, leaving the support posts for a guardrail dangling above a washout with a near-vertical face 60 feet high and nearly 150 feet wide. The park service plans to have the washout repaired and the entire parkway between US 321 and US 129 open by June 2004.

17.5 Pass a pullout by a sign for the Foothills Parkway on the left.

17.7 Reach the end of the ride at the junction with US 129 next to Chilhowee Lake, which is an impoundment of the Little Tennessee River.
The junction of US 129 and US 411, in Maryville, Tennessee, is 22 miles to the right. Fontana, North Carolina, is 25 miles to the left via US 129 and NC 28. US 129 from this junction to the Tennessee state line is called Tail of the Dragon by motorcyclists who cherish its endless twists and turns.

Short and Sweet: Since there is little level riding along this route, try starting at Look Rock Picnic Area and riding 9.6 downhill miles to US 321.

For Extra Credit: Strong riders can go 35.4 miles round trip. Another option is to ride the incomplete section of the Foothills Parkway east of Walland. This section begins at the gate to the left of the bottom of the access ramp for the parkway. This rough paved road extends 9.8 miles east to a dead end just beyond a pair of bridges that mark the start of the "missing link." Until the link is compete the Park Service has closed the road to vehicles, but it is open to hikers, cyclists, and horseback riders. Mountain bikes are the best bet on this ride. This section will be closed if any new construction begins.

11

Little River

- **DISTANCE:** A 17.8-mile round-trip ride. The Short and Sweet version is 8.9 miles one way. The Extra Credit ride is a 27.3-mile round trip.
- **TERRAIN:** Flat riding on low-traffic paved roads alongside the Little River.
- **SPECIAL FEATURES:** Rapids and cabins along the Little River.
- **GENERAL LOCATION:** The ride connects the communities of Maryville and Townsend, Tennessee.
- **MAPS:** Hiking and Biking on the Peaceful Side of the Smokies.
- **ACCESS:** From the intersection of US 321 and US 35 (Washington Street) in Maryville, Tennessee, follow US 321N toward Townsend and Great Smoky Mountains National Park. US 321 is also called Lamar Alexander Parkway. Turn left on Tuckaleechee Pike at 4.8 miles. Drive past Heritage High School to reach Coulter Bridge at the intersection of Old Walland Highway and Ellejoy Road at 6.5 miles. To begin the ride, turn right on Old Walland Highway.

Of all the streams draining the Tennessee side of Great Smoky Mountains National Park, the Little River is one of the prettiest and a favorite of outdoor enthusiasts. The river sections in the park and in nearby Townsend are favorites with tubers who find the rapids a good mix of fun and adventure. The banks of the upper reaches in the national park can be crowded with fishermen.

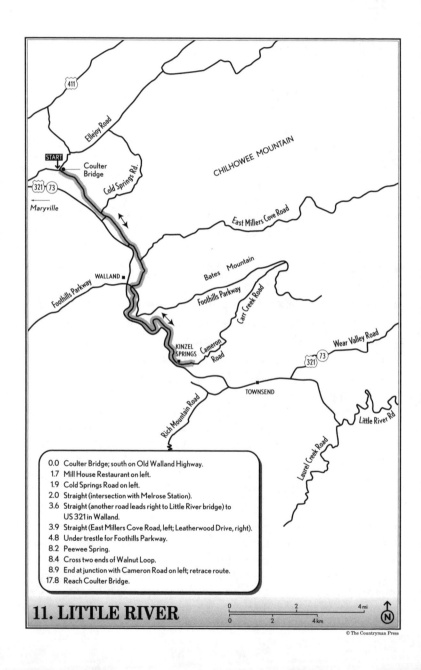

0.0 Coulter Bridge; south on Old Walland Highway.
1.7 Mill House Restaurant on left.
1.9 Cold Springs Road on left.
2.0 Straight (intersection with Melrose Station).
3.6 Straight (another road leads right to Little River bridge) to
      US 321 in Walland.
3.9 Straight (East Millers Cove Road, left; Leatherwood Drive, right).
4.8 Under trestle for Foothills Parkway.
8.2 Peewee Spring.
8.4 Cross two ends of Walnut Loop.
8.9 End at junction with Cameron Road on left; retrace route.
17.8 Reach Coulter Bridge.

11. LITTLE RIVER

0   2   4 mi
0   2   4 km

The riding along the river between Townsend and Maryville is a favorite also. On the east side of the river is Old Walland Highway, a narrow, low-traffic road favored by cyclists. On the west side of the river is US 321, a high-volume, high-speed, four-lane road with a wide shoulder. Though the Tennessee Department of Transportation has designated US 321 as a bike route, almost no one rides there. Old Walland Highway offers a quiet, safe alternative without the constant buzz of speeding traffic. Like most rural roads in Tennessee, Old Walland Highway has no shoulder, and there are a few spots where visibility is limited. But this road sees much bike traffic, and most drivers are considerate of cyclists.

The calm, quiet of the Little River is a reflection of the area around it. In contrast to the highly commercialized and over-developed gateway communities of Cherokee, Gatlinburg, Pigeon Forge, and Sevierville, Townsend calls itself the peaceful side of the Smokies. The recent widening of US 321 through town will undoubtedly prompt some new development, but so far the outlet malls, theme parks, and pervasive tackiness of Pigeon Forge have been kept away.

The widening of US 321 brought with it some benefits for cyclists. There is now a popular bike path, called the Townsend Bicycle Trail, situated on both sides of the highway from Old Walland Highway Bridge, near the turnaround point of this ride, to the south end of town near the boundary with Great Smoky Mountains National Park called the Townsend Bicycle Trail. There are parking areas for trail users near both ends of the path.

0.0 From Coulter Bridge, ride south on Old Walland Highway.
The ride begins in open farmland.

1.7 Pass the Mill House Restaurant on the left.
A small dam in the river once powered the mill.

1.9 Pass Cold Springs Road on the left.

2.0 Go straight through the intersection with Melrose Station.
A bridge to the right on Melrose Station Road leads to US 321 near milepost 20.
The steep slopes of Chilhowee Mountain loom above farmland along the river.

3.6 Continue straight (where another road leads right to a bridge over the Little River) to US 321 in the community of Walland by a gas station and the fire station.

Here the ride enters the narrow gorge that the Little River has cut through Chilhowee Mountain. The river changes from placid flatwater to a lively mountain stream.

3.9 Go straight where East Millers Cove Road leads left and then Leatherwood Drive leads right.

4.8 Pass underneath a mammoth trestle for the Foothills Parkway.
The section above you is the incomplete and closed road leading east from Walland toward Wear Valley. Just beyond, nestled against the south slope of Chilhowee Mountain, is Camp Wesley Woods, operated by the United Methodist Church. The riverbanks ahead are dominated by a community of riverside retreats.

The Little River ride keeps in close touch with its namesake

The cabins range from those that turn you green with envy to those turning green with mold.

8.2 Peewee Spring pours sweet water from a pipe on the bank of the river.

8.4 In the middle of a community dominated by summer cabins, cross the two ends of Walnut Loop.

8.9 Reach the end of the ride at a junction with Cameron Road on the left and a narrow concrete bridge leading right to US 321 and the Townsend bike paths.
Retrace your route to return to the parking area.

17.8 Reach the parking area at Coulter Bridge.

Short and Sweet: Get a car shuttle and ride the route one way for 8.9 miles. Or, make a loop of the Townsend Bicycle Trail paths for a 9.5-mile ride.

For Extra Credit: Add a loop around the Townsend Bicycle Trail for a 27.3-mile ride.

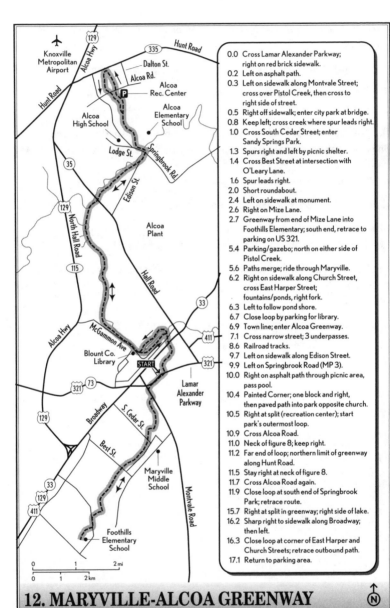

0.0 Cross Lamar Alexander Parkway; right on red brick sidewalk.
0.2 Left on asphalt path.
0.3 Left on sidewalk along Montvale Street; cross over Pistol Creek, then cross to right side of street.
0.5 Right off sidewalk; enter city park at bridge.
0.8 Keep left; cross creek where spur leads right.
1.0 Cross South Cedar Street; enter Sandy Springs Park.
1.3 Spurs right and left by picnic shelter.
1.4 Cross Best Street at intersection with O'Leary Lane.
1.6 Spur leads right.
2.0 Short roundabout.
2.4 Left on sidewalk at monument.
2.6 Right on Mize Lane.
2.7 Greenway from end of Mize Lane into Foothills Elementary; south end, retrace to parking on US 321.
5.4 Parking/gazebo; north on either side of Pistol Creek.
5.6 Paths merge; ride through Maryville.
6.2 Right on sidewalk along Church Street, cross East Harper Street; fountains/ponds, right fork.
6.3 Left to follow pond shore.
6.7 Close loop by parking for library.
6.9 Town line; enter Alcoa Greenway.
7.1 Cross narrow street; 3 underpasses.
8.6 Railroad tracks.
9.7 Left on sidewalk along Edison Street.
9.9 Left on Springbrook Road (MP 3).
10.0 Right on asphalt path through picnic area, pass pool.
10.4 Painted Corner; one block and right, then paved path into park opposite church.
10.5 Right at split (recreation center); start park's outermost loop.
10.9 Cross Alcoa Road.
11.0 Neck of figure 8; keep right.
11.2 Far end of loop; northern limit of greenway along Hunt Road.
11.5 Stay right at neck of figure 8.
11.7 Cross Alcoa Road again.
11.9 Close loop at south end of Springbrook Park; retrace route.
15.7 Right at split in greenway; right side of lake.
16.2 Sharp right to sidewalk along Broadway; then left.
16.3 Close loop at corner of East Harper and Church Streets; retrace outbound path.
17.1 Return to parking area.

12. MARYVILLE-ALCOA GREENWAY

Maryville-Alcoa Greenway

- **DISTANCE:** A 17.1-mile round-trip ride. The Short and Sweet version is 5.4 miles round trip. The Extra Credit ride is 34.2 miles round trip.
- **TERRAIN:** A generally flat, paved course through neighborhoods and parks in the neighboring towns of Maryville and Aloca.
- **SPECIAL FEATURES:** Bicentennial Greenbelt Park in Maryville and Springbrook Park in Alcoa.
- **GENERAL LOCATION:** Through the towns of Alcoa and Maryville in Tennessee.
- **MAPS:** The Maryville-Alcoa Greenway map is available from the towns of Maryville or Alcoa, and from Blount County.
- **ACCESS:** There are several trailheads for the greenway. One of the easiest to find is located 0.4 mile west of the intersection of Washington Street (TN 35) and Lamar Alexander Parkway (US 321) in Maryville. At this intersection, turn west on US 321, go through one stop light at Court Street, and look for a parking area by a gazebo on your right. The north end of the greenway can be reached by taking Hunt Road Exit off US 129 just south of Knoxville's McGee-Tyson Airport. Turn right off Hunt Road in 0.8 mile on Dalton Street. Turn left on Alcoa Road and go one block, then turn right again on Dalton Street to reach the parking area at Springbrook Recreation Center.

The adjacent towns of Maryville and Alcoa have pooled resources to construct one of the region's finest, and longest, greenways. The popular 9-mile greenway attracts cyclists, runners, and fitness walkers from both in, and out of, town. Here is the chance to explore the neighborhoods, parks, and downtown areas of both towns at a leisurely pace. This is the type of fun, easy riding where lunch deserves to be a tasty picnic basket, not just a few energy bars.

The greenway extends from Foothills Elementary School in Maryville north to Springbrook Park in Alcoa. There are parking and access points at Foothills Elementary School, Sandy Springs Park, Bicentennial Greenbelt Park, Alcoa Elementary School, and Springbrook Recreation Center, as well as at a number of other smaller areas. The Lamar Alexander Parkway access is relatively easy to find, is not heavily used on weekends, and has some shaded parking spots. Our route will start near the middle of the greenway and include out-and-back trips to the south end at Foothills Elementary School and to the north end at Springbrook Park. This gives riders the option of riding 5.4, 12, or 17.1 miles and a chance to stop by their car along the way for anything they might have forgotten.

0.0 From the parking area, cross Lamar Alexander Parkway and turn right on a red brick sidewalk.
The greenway in Maryville is marked at 0.25-mile intervals.

0.2 Turn left off the sidewalk on an asphalt path.

0.3 Turn left on a sidewalk along Montvale Street, cross over Pistol Creek, and then cross to the right side of the street, opposite Magnolia Cemetery at the intersection with Goddard Avenue.

0.5 Turn right off the sidewalk and enter a city park at a bridge over Pistol Creek.

0.8 Keep left and cross the creek where a spur trail leads right.
The greenway includes a number of short spurs that lead to small parking areas or neighborhood access points. On your first trip, these spurs may seem confusing, but if you come to a point where the greenway seems to prematurely end, just return to the last split and continue on the main path.

Duck ponds and fountains are the highlight of Maryville's Greenbelt Park

1.0 Cross South Cedar Street by some tennis courts and enter Sandy Springs Park.

1.3 Ignore spur trails leading right and left by a picnic shelter.

1.4 Cross Best Street at the intersection with O'Leary Lane.
Here the greenway enters pretty park land alongside Pistol Creek.

1.6 A spur trail leads right.

2.0 The greenway enters a short roundabout.

2.4 Turn left on a sidewalk at a monument, which was dedicated in 1996 to Margaret Stevenson, and climb alongside Montgomery Lane.
Stevenson's many climbs of Mount LeConte in Great Smoky Mountains National Park, at an age when most people have long since retired their walking shoes, have made her the community's best-known walker. Appropriately, the view ahead extends to the foothills of the Great Smoky Mountains.

2.6 Turn right on Mize Lane.
This short hill is the only steep climb along the greenway.

2.7 Follow the greenway from the end of Mize Lane into the parking area for Foothills Elementary School and the south end of the greenway.
The school is a good vantage point for enjoying the views of the Great Smoky Mountains before retracing your route back to the parking area on US 321.

5.4 From the parking area and gazebo, ride north on either of two branches on opposite sides of Pistol Creek.

5.6 The paths merge on the right side of the creek.
For the next mile you will ride through the heart of downtown Maryville. The greenway will pass through two huge culverts below stone bridges as it traces a rolling path. There are many spur trails here; always keep to the main path along the creek. An energetic spring marks the site of Fort Craig. The fort, one of the earliest settlements in Blount County, was built in 1785 and covered 2.2 acres.

6.2 Turn right on a sidewalk along Church Street and soon cross East Harper Street.
Here the greenway splits to go around a series of fountains and duck ponds in Bicentennial Greenbelt Park. Take the right fork of the greenway along Church Street.

6.3 Turn left off Church Street to follow the shore of the pond.

6.7 Close the loop at the end of the ponds by the parking area for the Blount County Library.

6.9 Reach the Alcoa-Maryville town line and enter the town of Alcoa portion of greenway.
In Alcoa the greenway is marked at 0.5-mile intervals and the numbers reset to 0 at the line. The first few miles contain some interpretive displays. If the town's name sounds familiar to you, it may be because Alcoa is a company town, named for the firm that may have forged your aluminum frame.

7.1 Cross a narrow street.
The next few miles of flat, wide open trail are the only areas where fast riding is safe, or possible. Three underpasses below Bessemer Street, Calderwood Street, and Hall Road (TN 35) make this a fun, traffic-free stretch.

7.3 Pass a spur trail to the left and enter open park land.

7.9 Pass a parking area on the left.

8.6 Cross some railroad tracks near a lumberyard. A sign reminds us of the obvious fact that trail users should yield to trains.
The greenway then passes behind the US Foodservice distribution center, enters a wooded area, and passes underneath a railroad trestle.

9.7 Turn left on a sidewalk along Edison Street.

9.9 Turn left on Springbrook Road near milepost 3.
Milepost 3 is the last milepost along the trail. Markings for the greenway end at this point. With some careful navigating you can follow the route of the greenway into Springbrook Park and ride a narrow loop through one of Alcoa's prettiest neighborhoods.

10.0 Turn right off Springbrook Road by The Park at Duck Pond and a picnic area in front of Alcoa Elementary School.
Follow an asphalt path through the picnic area to a parking area beside the Alcoa public pool. Continue past the pool alongside a sidewalk.

10.4 Reach the corner where Vose Road, Faraday Street, and Darwin Street intersect near Alcoa High School.
The sidewalks here have been painted with an array of slogans and symbols, presumably by the local school kids. Go right one block from "Painted Corner" and then take the paved path into the park opposite First United Methodist Church.

10.5 Go right at a split at Springbrook Recreation Center and the start of the trails at Springbrook .
A map board at the center shows the trails through the park. Faded paint marks designate a series of four loops in the park. Our route will follow the outermost loop.

10.9 Cross Alcoa Road.
This pretty park features a fountain with benches and an impressive statue of a black bear carved into the stump of one of the park's trees.

11.0 The trails narrow into the neck of a figure eight.
Keep right and climb a small hill.

11.2 Reach the far end of the loop and the northern limit of the greenway alongside Hunt Road.

11.5 Stay right at the neck of the figure 8.

11.7 Cross Alcoa Road again.

11.9 Close the loop at the south end of Springbrook Park.
From this point retrace your route back to the parking area at the near end of Bicentennial Greenbelt Park across from the library.

15.7 Go right at the split in the greenway to stay on the right side of the lake.
The greenway splits again to form two parallel paths around the lake. Both paths lead to the same place.

16.2 Make a sharp, steep right turn toward a sidewalk along Broadway.
Turn left on the sidewalk.

16.3 Reach the corner of East Harper and Church Streets at the end of the loop.
Retrace your outbound path to return to the parking area.

17.1 Return to the parking area.

Short and Sweet: For a quick introduction to the greenway, try riding the 5.4-mile round trip from the parking area south to Foothills Elementary School.

For Extra Credit: There is no easy way to extend the ride beyond doing two laps for 34.2 miles. However, both US 321 (leading south of Maryville toward Townsend) and US 411 (leading west from Maryville) are wide four-lane highways with ample shoulders for cyclists.

13

House Mountain

- **DISTANCE:** A 27.9-mile loop. The Short and Sweet version is a 14.4-mile loop. The Extra Credit ride is 49.1 miles.

- **TERRAIN:** The ride is on low-traffic, paved country roads over hilly terrain.

- **SPECIAL FEATURES:** The loop circles House Mountain State Natural Area and the highest point in Knox County.

- **GENERAL LOCATION:** 13 miles east of Knoxville.

- **MAPS:** The *Tennessee Atlas and Gazetteer* (DeLorme) shows the roads the route travels. The Smoky Mountain Wheelmen web site contains maps of two alternate versions of this ride.

- **ACCESS:** From I-40 on the east side of Knoxville, take Exit 392 at Rutledge Pike and drive east on US 11W. After a stop light below the I-640 overpass at 2.4 miles, US 11W becomes a bike route with a wide shoulder. Pass East Knox Elementary School at 9.8 miles, then turn left on Idumea Road at 11.4 miles, where there normally is a sign for House Mountain. Turn left on Hogskin Road at 12.1 miles and reach the small gravel parking area for House Mountain at 13 miles.

The House Mountain ride traverses the remarkably pretty northeast corner of Knox County. Here small farms still outnumber encroaching subdivisions, and both traffic and the pace of life run a little slower than they do in town. The route is laced with views of dramatic House Mountain, as well as McAnnally Ridge to the

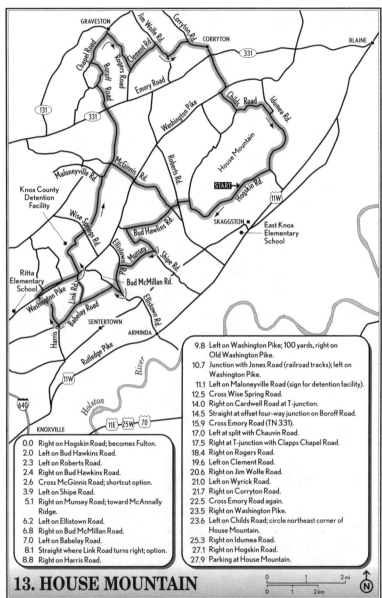

GRAVESTON

Jim Wolfe Rd.

Corryton Rd.

CORRYTON

BLAINE

Chapel Road

Rogers Road

Clement Rd.

331

Boruff Road

Emory Road

131

331

Washington Pike

Childs Road

Idumea Rd.

McGinnis Rd.

Maloneyville Rd.

Knox County
Detention
Facility

Wise Springs Rd.

Roberts Rd.

House Mountain

START →

Hogskin Rd.

11W

Bud Hawlins Rd.

Ellistown Rd.

Munsey

Shipe Rd.

SKAGGSTON

East Knox
Elementary
School

Ritta
Elementary
School

Washington Pike

Link Rd.

Babelay Road

Bud McMillan Rd.

Ellistown Rd.

SENTERTOWN

Harris

ARMINDA

Rutledge Pike

11W

River

Holston

640

KNOXVILLE

11E — 25W — 70

0.0 Right on Hogskin Road; becomes Fulton.
2.0 Left on Bud Hawkins Road.
2.3 Left on Roberts Road.
2.4 Right on Bud Hawkins Road.
2.6 Cross McGinnis Road; shortcut option.
3.9 Left on Shipe Road.
5.1 Right on Munsey Road; toward McAnnally Ridge.
6.2 Left on Ellistown Road.
6.8 Right on Bud McMillan Road.
7.0 Left on Babelay Road.
8.1 Straight where Link Road turns right; option.
8.8 Right on Harris Road.

9.8 Left on Washington Pike; 100 yards, right on Old Washington Pike.
10.7 Junction with Jones Road (railroad tracks); left on Washington Pike.
11.1 Left on Maloneyville Road (sign for detention facility).
12.5 Cross Wise Spring Road.
14.0 Right on Cardwell Road at T-junction.
14.5 Straight at offset four-way junction on Boroff Road.
15.9 Cross Emory Road (TN 331).
17.0 Left at split with Chauvin Road.
17.5 Right at T-junction with Clapps Chapel Road.
18.4 Right on Rogers Road.
19.6 Left on Clement Road.
20.6 Right on Jim Wolfe Road.
21.0 Left on Wyrick Road.
21.7 Right on Corryton Road.
22.5 Cross Emory Road again.
23.5 Right on Washington Pike.
23.6 Left on Childs Road; circle northeast corner of House Mountain.
25.3 Right on Idumea Road.
27.1 Right on Hogskin Road.
27.9 Parking at House Mountain.

13. HOUSE MOUNTAIN

0   1   2 mi
0   1   2 km

N

© The Countryman Press

south and Clinch Mountain to the east. Barns, working and other-wise, dot the small valley farms and include a wide array of building styles. Likewise, each small community has its own small church, built in its own unique style.

Like many rural roads, traffic conditions here can vary. But as long as you avoid the after-work hours, you will not see too many speeding cars. You also should be prepared for a few neighborhood dogs. Just where and when you might be chased depends on who is napping, how hot it is, or just how close it is to feeding time. But most of the local dogs don't have a lot of skill chasing bikes and can be easily deterred by a quick squirt with your water bottle. For my first few years in Knoxville, I lived in the nearby Three Points community and these roads were frequently included in my after-work ride. I had no serious problems with cars or dogs on the bike, but conditions may change and it is always best to be alert to your surroundings.

In the summer of 2002, nearly all the road signs along this route were in place. Since this crop of signs won't be in place forever, I've described the loop assuming that no signs will be in place for your ride. To save space I've also omitted a small number of intersections that you will ride straight through.

House Mountain was established as a State Natural Area in 1987. The 500-acre park was acquired through donations from a local landowner and the Trust for Public Land and then donated to the state. Because there is little room on the property for facilities, the state has been an unenthusiastic landowner. However, the donation of a smaller parcel of land with access to Hogskin Road allowed the opening of the park in 1993. Volunteers constructed 5 miles of hiking trail leading to overlooks at the east and west ends of the mountain. The park has been a local favorite ever since.

In 2001, Governor Don Sundquist chose House Mountain as one of the targets for his state parks closures, despite the park's measly $900 budget the previous year. Management has since been assumed by Knox County Parks and Recreation, who continues to operate it as a hiking and natural area. The parking area is open dawn to dusk seven days a week. There are no other facilities at the area.

One of the many scenic farms in the shadow of House Mountain

0.0 From the parking area, turn right on Hogskin Road, which will become Fulton Road.

2.0 Turn left on Bud Hawkins Road.

2.3 Turn left on Roberts Road.

2.4 Turn right on Bud Hawkins Road.
Look behind you for a nice view of the west end of House Mountain.

2.6 Cross McGinnis Road.
At this point the ride joins a loop that was once marked with orange paint by the Smoky Mountain Wheelmen, but as of 2003, no paint was visible. If you'd like to shortcut the main loop, turn right and ride 2.1 miles to Boroff Road and rejoin the ride at the 14.5-mile point. Rejoining the ride at this point will make an 18.1-mile loop.

3.9 Turn left on Shipe Road.

5.1 Turn right on Munsey Road and head toward McAnnally Ridge.

6.2 Turn left on Ellistown Road.
Ellistown Road has a yellow center line and a bit more traffic, but the ride is all downhill.

6.8 Turn right on Bud McMillan Road.

7.0 Turn left on Babelay Road.

8.1 Continue straight where Link Road turns right.
If you are unwilling to try your luck with a very short section of high-speed traffic on Washington Pike, turn right here and follow Link Road for 0.9 mile to Washington Pike. Almost immediately across is the intersection with Maloneyville Road, where you can rejoin the ride at the 11.1-mile point, saving 2.1 miles.

8.8 Turn right on Harris Road.

9.8 Turn left on Washington Pike.
In about 100 yards, Old Washington Pike will intersect on the far side. Turn right on Old Washington Pike. Watch for a crossing of railroad tracks. A short distance to the left on Washington Pike is Ritta Elementary School, an alternate starting point.

10.7 At a junction with Jones Road and the railroad tracks, turn left on Washington Pike.
Be careful in traffic.

11.1 Turn left on Maloneyville Road at a prominent sign for Knox County Detention Facility.
You will ride past the detention facility and cross the railroad tracks again.

12.5 Cross Wise Springs Road.

14.0 Turn right on Cardwell Road at a T-junction.
Cardwell Road marks the return to pretty country roads similar to those at the start of the ride.

14.5 Go straight through an offset four-way junction on Boroff Road.
McGinnis Road enters on the right and Booher Road enters on the left.

15.9 Cross Emory Road, which is TN 331.

17.0 Bear left at a split with Chauvin Road.

17.5 Go right at a T-junction with Clapps Chapel Road at Bethel Baptist Church.

18.4 Turn right on Rogers Road.

19.6 Turn left on Clement Road.
Just beyond this intersection are views of the north side of House Mountain.

20.6 Turn right on Jim Wolfe Road.

21.0 Turn left on Wyrick Road.

21.7 Turn right on Corryton Road.
Straight ahead are views of Clinch Mountain. One of the most prominent features of the Tennessee Valley, Clinch Mountain extends as a long, narrow ridge north-east into Virginia. As you ride though the community of Corryton, keep on the main road at all junctions. The road will bend south, guiding you back toward House Mountain.

22.5 Cross Emory Road (TN 331).
Even though Corryton Elementary School is on this road, traffic can be moving at high speeds.

23.5 Turn right on Washington Pike.

23.6 Turn left on Childs Road and begin to circle around the northeast corner of House Mountain.
The ride leaves the Smoky Mountain Wheelmen's course at this point.

25.3 Turn right on Idumea Road and begin a steep climb.

27.1 Turn right on Hogskin Road and climb to the parking area.

27.9 Reach the House Mountain parking area.

Short and Sweet: Ritta Elementary School is only 0.2 mile east on Washington Pike from the intersection with Harris Road. To ride only the west part of the loop, park at Ritta Elementary School and ride east to join the loop at the junction of Washington Pike and Old Washington Pike. Leave the route at the 14.5-mile mark by making a right turn on McGinnis Road. Ride 2.1

miles on McGinnis Road and join the loop again at the 2.6-mile point. This loop will be 14.4 miles long.

For Extra Credit: Try starting your ride at East Knox Elementary School on US 11W and riding to the House Mountain parking area. Returning the same way will make your entire ride 49.1 miles.

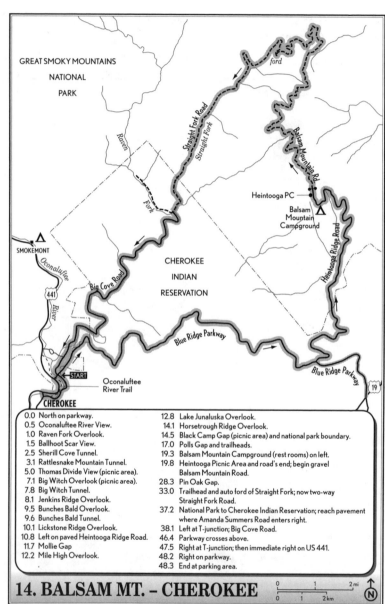

GREAT SMOKY MOUNTAINS
NATIONAL
PARK

Straight Fork Road

Straight Fork

Raven

Fork

ford

Balsam Mountain Rd

Heintooga PC

Balsam
Mountain
Campground

Heintooga Ridge Road

SMOKEMONT

Oconaluftee

CHEROKEE
INDIAN
RESERVATION

Big Cove Road

(441)

River

Blue Ridge Parkway

Blue Ridge Parkway

19

START

Oconaluftee
River Trail

CHEROKEE

0.0 North on parkway.	12.8 Lake Junaluska Overlook.
0.5 Oconaluftee River View.	14.1 Horsetrough Ridge Overlook.
1.0 Raven Fork Overlook.	14.5 Black Camp Gap (picnic area) and national park boundary.
1.5 Ballhoot Scar View.	17.0 Polls Gap and trailheads.
2.5 Sherill Cove Tunnel.	19.3 Balsam Mountain Campground (rest rooms) on left.
3.1 Rattlesnake Mountain Tunnel.	19.8 Heintooga Picnic Area and road's end; begin gravel
5.0 Thomas Divide View (picnic area).	Balsam Mountain Road.
7.1 Big Witch Overlook (picnic area).	28.3 Pin Oak Gap.
7.8 Big Witch Tunnel.	33.0 Trailhead and auto ford of Straight Fork; now two-way
8.1 Jenkins Ridge View.	Straight Fork Road.
9.5 Bunches Bald Overlook.	37.2 National Park to Cherokee Indian Reservation; reach pavement
9.6 Bunches Bald Tunnel.	where Amanda Summers Road enters right.
10.1 Lickstone Ridge View.	38.1 Left at T-junction; Big Cove Road.
10.8 Left on paved Heintooga Ridge Road.	46.4 Parkway crosses above.
11.7 Mollie Gap	47.5 Right at T-junction; then immediate right on US 441.
12.2 Mile High Overlook.	48.2 Right on parkway.
	48.3 End at parking area.

14. BALSAM MT. – CHEROKEE

0		1		2 mi
0	1		2 km	

N

© The Countryman Press

Balsam Mountain–Cherokee

- **DISTANCE:** The loop is 48.3 miles around. The Short and Sweet version is 8 miles round trip. The Extra Credit ride is 53.1 miles.

- **TERRAIN:** The ride is a mix of paved and well-maintained gravel roads along the Blue Ridge Parkway and through Great Smoky Mountains National Park. There is 3,300 feet of climbing to reach Heintooga Picnic Area. The rest of the ride is all downhill. There are five tunnels on this section of the Blue Ridge Parkway, plus a normally shallow ford of Straight Fork.

- **SPECIAL FEATURES:** The route travels a remote corner of Great Smoky Mountains National Park on roads ideal for wildlife watching or enjoying fall colors. The lower reaches follow the Straight and Raven Forks of the Oconaluftee River through the Cherokee Indian Reservation.

- **GENERAL LOCATION:** The ride begins near the town of Cherokee, North Carolina.

- **MAPS:** Both the Great Smoky Mountains Official Map and Guide and the Blue Ridge Parkway Official Map and Guide issued by the National Park Service show this ride.

- **ACCESS:** The Blue Ridge Parkway begins on US 441, 0.8 mile south of Oconaluftee Visitor Center and 0.7 mile north of Big Cove Road in Cherokee. There is a gravel pullout at 0.1 mile, near a parkway sign immediately after the parkway crosses above the Oconaluftee River and Big Cove Road.

The longest and hardest ride in this book covers a smorgasbord of terrain on the North Carolina side of Great Smoky Mountains National Park. The ride begins where the Blue Ridge Parkway starts on the Cherokee Indian Reservation and climbs the parkway to Heintooga Ridge Road. Heintooga Ridge Road leads into Great Smoky Mountains National Park where the route follows the one-way gravel Balsam Mountain Road to the gravel Straight Fork Road. Straight Fork Road leads into the town of Cherokee, North Carolina, and back to the parkway.

Bikepackers can make an overnight trip by spending the night at Balsam Mountain Campground, 19 miles into the route. Expect a brutal first day of climbing on paved roads but an easy, all downhill second day on mostly gravel roads. Balsam Mountain and Straight Fork Roads are closed to vehicles during the winter. However, cyclists, hikers, and horseback riders can use the roads year-round.

The Smokies is the most heavily visited national park in the country, and the Blue Ridge Parkway is the most visited area managed by the Park Service. But most visitors stay far from this loop. By parkway standards, the southern end is relatively quiet, and the Balsam Mountain area is one of the Smokies' quietest corners. Since Balsam Mountain Road is one-way, gravel, and too narrow for oversized vehicles, you may not see another vehicle along its entire length.

0.0 Begin riding north on the Blue Ridge Parkway.
The ride begins with a long, 3,000-foot climb.

0.5 Pass Oconaluftee River View (2,200 feet) on the left.
Great Smoky Mountains National Park covers over 500,000 acres of lush forest unrivaled in the East for beauty and diversity. The Smokies contain more species of trees than can be found on the entire European continent. With 3,000 feet of climbing and several ecosystems ahead of you, it's likely that you'll see most of them. The high peak in the background is Newton Bald. Like many mountaintops around the park, this bald is now completed covered with mature trees.

1.0 Pass Raven Fork Overlook (2,400 feet) on the left.

Raven Fork and Straight Fork are the two main streams that come together to feed the Oconaluftee River. You will ride beside both forks near the end of the loop.

1.5 Pass Ballhoot Scar View (2,550 feet) on the left.
Ballhooting was a logger's term for recovering logs by simply rolling or sliding them down a hillside. While the environmental damage of this practice is still visible today, you can't help but imagine the logs themselves fared little better.

2.5 Enter Sherill Cove Tunnel.
Be very careful to avoid traffic in this long curving tunnel.

3.1 Enter Rattlesnake Mountain Tunnel.
This tunnel also curves but is short.

5.0 Pass Thomas Divide View (3,735 feet) and a picnic area on the left.
Thomas Divide is the long ridge that US 441 uses to begin its descent from Newfound Gap to Cherokee.

6.7 Pass the gated, gravel Road 406 on the right, which leads to Barnett Knob Fire Tower.
Begin a short, but well-deserved, downhill ride here.

7.1 Pass Big Witch Overlook (4,160 feet) and a picnic area on the left.
Just beyond the overlook, the parkway reaches the crest of the Balsam Mountains and an unsigned gravel road leading left to Bunches Creek. Beyond the crest, the road resumes its climb.

7.8 Enter Big Witch Tunnel.
This tunnel is also short but has a slight curve.

8.1 Pass Jenkins Ridge Overlook (4,445 feet) on the right.

9.5 Pass Bunches Bald Overlook (4,923 feet) on the right.

9.6 Enter the short Bunches Bald Tunnel.

10.1 Pass Lickstone Ridge Overlook (5,150 feet) on the right.
An interpretive sign explains the history of the Cherokee Indian Reservation. Just ahead is another short tunnel and finally some downhill riding.

10.8 Turn left off the parkway on the paved Heintooga Ridge Road, which here is administered by the Blue Ridge Parkway.

The speed limit on Heintooga Ridge Road is 35 mph. A sign indicates that it is 3.6 miles to Black Camp Gap, 8 miles to Balsam Mountain Campground, and 9 miles to Heintooga Picnic Area. The road soon crosses two unsigned gravel roads. Begin climbing through a northern hardwood forest where beech and maple trees are common.

11.7 Reach Mollie Gap (5,352 feet).
A gravel road to the left leads to a commercial campground.

12.2 Reach Mile High Overlook (only 5,250 feet).
To the right is the town of Maggie Valley. Begin another descent here.

12.8 Pass Lake Junaluska Overlook (5,034 feet) on the right.

14.1 Pass Horsetrough Ridge Overlook (4,540 feet) on the right.

The auto ford of Straight Fork at Round Bottoms can be dangerous in high water.

14.5 Reach Black Camp Gap (4,466 feet) and the boundary of Great Smoky Mountains National Park.

At the gap, there is a picnic area and the Masonic Monument, where North Carolina masons have met yearly since 1935. The monument is constructed of rocks imported from 41 states, many countries, and every continent. Begin climbing, again.

16.1 Reach a dirt pullout that marks the end of Flat Creek Trail.

The trail leads 0.7 mile to the scenic Flat Creek Falls and another 1.9 miles to Heintooga Picnic Area.

17.0 Reach Polls Gap and trailheads for Rough Fork and Hemphill Bald Trails.

As of 2003, the badly eroded Polls Gap Trail was closed and not expected to reopen soon.

18.8 Pass a gated gravel road on the left.

19.3 Reach the entrance to Balsam Mountain Campground on the left.

One of the nicest campgrounds in the park, Balsam Mountain is open seasonally. There are 45 sites, including one area for tent camping only. The campground is rarely full, even on weekends. There is a rest room with water just a short ride into the campground.

19.8 Reach Heintooga Picnic Area and the end of Heintooga Ridge Road.

The picnic area marks the north end of Flat Creek Trail. Here also begins the gravel Balsam Mountain Road. The gate at the start of the road is locked from dusk to dawn. A sign at the start of the road indicates that Cherokee, North Carolina, is 28 miles and one hour away, a rather optimistic estimate for a road with a speed limit of 15 mph.

The character of the ride drastically changes at this point. Besides going from pavement to gravel, the road changes from little used to almost never used. The one-way traffic guarantees solitude. It is possible you'll see no other vehicles, and you might see more wildlife than people.

25.8 Pass the Spruce Mountain Trailhead on the right.

There is no longer a lookout tower on top of Spruce Mountain.

27.7 Pass the Palmer Creek Trailhead on the right.

28.3 Reach Pin Oak Gap and the start of Balsam Mountain Trail.

33.0 Reach the trailhead for the eastern branch of Beech Mountain Trail.
*Just beyond the trailhead is the Round Bottoms auto ford of Straight Fork. Under
normal conditions, water levels will be low enough for safe travel. However, during
the height of spring runoff, or after storms, the water may be too deep to cross
safely.*

*On the other side of the auto ford, two-way travel resumes on what is now
called Straight Fork Road. You'll follow alongside Straight Fork as it rushes toward
its meeting with Raven Fork. The gravel road is now wider, straighter, and more
heavily used.*

33.7 Pass Round Bottoms Horse Camp on the right.

34.6 Reach the Hyatt Ridge Trailhead on the right.

37.2 Just after passing out of Great Smoky Mountains National Park into the
Cherokee Indian Reservation (and passing a fish hatchery), reach a paved
road at a sign for Amanda Summers Road, which enters from the right.

38.1 Turn left at a T-junction and a stop sign.
*You are now on Big Cove Road, which follows the combined flow of the Raven and
Straight forks of the Oconaluftee River. You will ride past several small communities and a multitude of commercial campgrounds that crowd the banks of this
pretty river.*

46.4 After crossing back into Great Smoky Mountains National Park, reach
a bridge where the Blue Ridge Parkway crosses above Big Cove Road and
the Oconaluftee River.
*If you are tired of riding at this point or have been pedaling the last several hours
through driving rain like a certain guidebook author, you can climb a narrow, slip-
pery path up the bank of the overpass to the parkway where your vehicle should be
within sight ahead. If climbing the bank with your bike is too ignominious an end to
the ride, you can brave the final 2 miles into Cherokee.*

47.5 Go right at a stop sign and a T-junction in the heart of the touristy part of
Cherokee. Then go immediately right again on US 441 toward the Smokies.

48.2 Turn right on the Blue Ridge Parkway.

48.3 Reach the end of the ride at the parking area.

Short and Sweet: There is no way to cut this loop short. If you're looking for
an easy out-and-back ride, start from the end of Big Cove Road and ride to

the auto ford at Raven Fork for an 8-mile round trip. Another option is the 1.5-mile Oconaluftee River Trail, which connects Oconaluftee Visitor Center with Cherokee. It is one of only three park trails open to mountain bikers.

For Extra Credit: There are few options for extending this loop. You can continue on the Blue Ridge Parkway past Heintooga Ridge Road to Soco Gap, which adds another 4.8 miles and 800 feet of climbing.

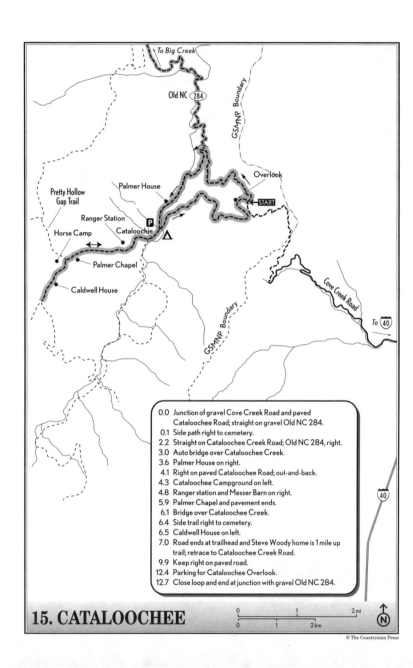

To Big Creek

Old NC 284

GSMNP Boundary

Overlook

Palmer House

←START

Pretty Hollow
Gap Trail

Ranger Station

Horse Camp

Cataloochie

P

△

Palmer Chapel

Caldwell House

Cove Creek Road

GSMNP Boundary

To 40

0.0 Junction of gravel Cove Creek Road and paved
     Cataloochee Road; straight on gravel Old NC 284.
0.1 Side path right to cemetery.
2.2 Straight on Cataloochee Creek Road; Old NC 284, right.
3.0 Auto bridge over Cataloochee Creek.
3.6 Palmer House on right.
4.1 Right on paved Cataloochee Road; out-and-back.
4.3 Cataloochee Campground on left.
4.8 Ranger station and Messer Barn on right.
5.9 Palmer Chapel and pavement ends.
6.1 Bridge over Cataloochee Creek.
6.4 Side trail right to cemetery.
6.5 Caldwell House on left.
7.0 Road ends at trailhead and Steve Woody home is 1 mile up
     trail; retrace to Cataloochee Creek Road.
9.9 Keep right on paved road.
12.4 Parking for Cataloochee Overlook.
12.7 Close loop and end at junction with gravel Old NC 284.

40

15. CATALOOCHEE

| 0 | | 1 | | 2 mi |
| 0 | 1 | | 2 km | |

N

Cataloochee

- **DISTANCE:** A 12.7-mile loop with a side trip. The Short and Sweet version is 5.8 miles round trip. The Extra Credit ride is 40.7 miles with a side trip.

- **TERRAIN:** A mix of gravel and paved roads within Great Smoky Mountains National Park that includes a 900-foot climb.

- **SPECIAL FEATURES:** A variety of historic buildings and the site of the park's experimental elk reintroduction.

- **GENERAL LOCATION:** About 14 miles west of Canton, North Carolina.

- **MAPS:** Great Smoky Mountains National Park Official Map and Guide is available at many locations around the park.

- **ACCESS:** Take Exit 20 for US 276 off I-40 in North Carolina. Immediately at the end of the off-ramp, turn right at a signed junction with Cove Creek Road. This narrow, winding road will climb for 4.7 miles before turning to gravel and becoming even steeper. At 5.9 miles, enter Great Smoky Mountains National Park at Cove Creek Gap. Drive another 1.9 miles down to the junction with the paved Cataloochee Road. You can park at this junction or turn left and drive 2.8 miles along your riding route to a small parking area near the junction with the gravel Cataloochee Creek Road.

Cataloochee Valley was once the most settled of all the areas now included in Great Smoky Mountains National Park. The valley's first permanent residents arrived in the 1830s, and within a few years, several small towns had developed along the valley floor. The residents mostly were farmers, but others worked for the logging operations that harvested the virgin timber on the mountain slopes. During the area's peak, over one thousand people lived here.

Residents of Cataloochee capitalized on the tourist trade even before the national park was established. Local families opened boarding houses for visitors attracted by the fishing, hiking, and horseback riding, and for those just looking to escape the hubbub of city life. The valley is remote and still remains one of the least visited parts of the Smokies. However, a 5-year experimental release of elk into Cataloochee has pulled in increasing numbers of visitors.

In 2001, the Park Service began the project to determine if elk can survive in the park permanently. These magnificent animals, once natives, were eliminated from the area by hunting and settlement over 150 years ago. Because Cataloochee is relatively isolated and has the proper mix of forest and open areas, the Park Service chose the valley to begin the experiment. Two releases have been conducted so far. The first group of 25 elk was brought in from the Land Between the Lakes National Recreation Area in western Tennessee and Kentucky. In 2002, more elk arrived from Canada's Elk Island National Park. Over 50 of the newcomers have prospered in the valley and produced a handful of young natives. The elk have dramatically increased visitation, especially in the fall when males begin to bugle as part of their courtship ritual. Some elk journeyed away from the valley to areas in Tennessee, Balsam Mountain, and the Cherokee Indian Reservation, but all have been returned to their new homes. The elk are most active near dawn and dusk in the grassy openings in the west end of the valley. Visitation and traffic in the valley are much heavier when the elk are active. If you ride the roads at the proper time, your chances are good of seeing a sight long absent from the Smokies.

Since Cataloochee is so remote, and you'll want to be riding near dusk or dawn to see the valley's elk, consider staying overnight in the campground, which is open mid-March through October.

0.0 At the junction of the gravel Cove Creek Road and the paved Cataloochee Road, go straight through the intersection along the gravel Old NC 284.

0.1 A rough path leads right about 0.5 mile to Hannah Hoglen Cemetery. *The road ahead offers fine views of Mount Sterling Ridge to the north. Enjoy the speedy descent along this well-maintained gravel road.*

2.2 Continue straight on Cataloochee Creek Road where Old NC 284 continues right.
Old NC 284 leads to the Little Cataloochee Trailhead in 3.6 miles, Big Creek in 14 miles, and Cosby in 26 miles.

3.0 Reach the end of the long descent at the auto bridge over Cataloochee Creek.

The bridge over Cataloochee Creek marks the end of a long downhill ride.

Just before the bridge, a closed side road leads right to some Park Service build-ings. On the far side of the bridge, another gated road leads right for about 0.3 mile along the creek.

3.6 Reach the Palmer House on the right.
This structure was built of logs in 1860 and remodeled with siding in 1902 at a time when there were over 700 people living in the valley. Three generations of Palmers prospered here from the 1850s to the 1930s. Jarvis Palmer added the tourist trade to the family's successful farming business. Guests came to fish along the creek, and took meals and lodging with the family. Jarvis built the cabin on the left side of the road in 1924. When Cataloochee became part of the park, the home was used as a ranger station.

4.1 Turn right on the paved Cataloochee Road to start the out-and-back leg of the ride.
Just beyond the junction is a small parking area on the left. Here you can pick up a brochure on the elk reintroduction, and for a small fee, get a copy of the Cataloochee Auto Tour booklet.

4.3 Cataloochee Campground is on the left.
The 27-site campground is closed from October 31st to March 15th, but the rest rooms are open year-round. Sites are $12 per night.

4.4 Pass the Caldwell Fork Trailhead on the left.
Despite its isolation, Cataloochee is one of the park areas most popular with horse-back riders, and the trails here show the wear of heavy horse traffic. If you'd like to avoid the horses on at least part of your hike and visit some virgin forest along the way, walk the 7.4-mile Boogerman Loop. Robert "Booger" Palmer never let the lumber companies take his trees and so left behind a beautiful forest intact for later visitors to enjoy.

4.8 Cataloochee Ranger Station and the Messer Barn are on the right.
The barn was moved here in 1977 from Little Cataloochee and restored. The road beyond this point is gated at night. You will shortly reach open meadows, which are the prime elk grazing areas.

5.9 Reach the Palmer Chapel and the end of the pavement.
This Methodist church was built around 1900. To the right a steep trail leads 400 feet to Palmer Cemetery. The families buried here include Messers, Caldwells, and Suttons, all of whom left their names on the map of the Smokies. At least two Confederate army veterans also lie here.

6.1 Reach the parking area for Cataloochee Horse Camp and Pretty Hollow Gap Trail at a bridge over Cataloochee Creek.
Across the bridge is a short side trail to Beech Grove School. This simple frame structure was built in 1901.

6.4 A side trail leads right to Hiram Caldwell Cemetery.
Hiram, his wife, Mary, and four other Caldwells are buried atop a small knoll.

6.5 Pass the Caldwell House on the left and the barn on the right.
When completed in 1906 Hiram Caldwell's home was one of the finest in the valley.

6.9 Pass the Big Fork Trailhead on the left.
A short distance up the trail are the acclimatization pens used to hold elk newly arrived at the park, before they are ready to be released into the wild.

7.0 Reach the end of the road at the Rough Creek Trailhead.
The Steve Woody home is 1 mile up this trail. You will now need to retrace your ride back to the intersection with Cataloochee Creek Road.

9.9 Keep right on the paved road at the intersection with the gravel Cataloochee Creek Road.
Your ride to this point has been either downhill or on gentle grades by the creek. Now, unfortunately, things are about to change. Cataloochee Overlook lies 900 feet above you. Though steep in places, the road is well graded and the views to be had from the overlook should take some of the sting out of the climb.

12.4 Reach the parking area for Cataloochee Overlook on the left.
From the overlook most of the high ridges surrounding the Cataloochee Valley can be seen. To the west are Balsam Mountain and its highpoint at Spruce Mountain. To the north is Mount Sterling Ridge. A magnificent lookout tower sits on top of Mount Sterling on the ridge's east end.

12.7 Close the loop and end your ride at the junction with the gravel Old NC 284.

Short and Sweet: Ride the valley floor from the parking area near the campground to the Rough Creek Trailhead and return for 5.8 easy miles.

For Extra Credit: Add the long ride up and over Mount Sterling Gap to Big Creek on Old NC 284 for an extra 28 miles round trip.

THE
BLUE RIDGE

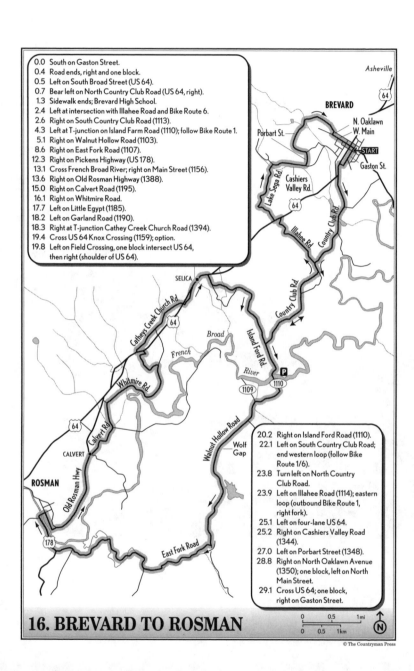

0.0 South on Gaston Street.
0.4 Road ends, right and one block.
0.5 Left on South Broad Street (US 64).
0.7 Bear left on North Country Club Road (US 64, right).
1.3 Sidewalk ends; Brevard High School.
2.4 Left at intersection with Illahee Road and Bike Route 6.
2.6 Right on South Country Club Road (1113).
4.3 Left at T-junction on Island Farm Road (1110); follow Bike Route 1.
5.1 Right on Walnut Hollow Road (1103).
8.6 Right on East Fork Road (1107).
12.3 Right on Pickens Highway (US 178).
13.1 Cross French Broad River; right on Main Street (1156).
13.6 Right on Old Rosman Highway (1388).
15.0 Right on Calvert Road (1195).
16.1 Right on Whitmire Road.
17.7 Left on Little Egypt (1185).
18.2 Left on Garland Road (1190).
18.3 Right at T-junction Cathey Creek Church Road (1394).
19.4 Cross US 64 Knox Crossing (1159); option.
19.8 Left on Field Crossing, one block intersect US 64,
       then right (shoulder of US 64).

Asheville

64

BREVARD

N. Oaklawn
W. Main

Porbart St.

START

Gaston St.

Lake Sega Rd.

Cashiers
Valley Rd.

64

Illahee Rd.

Country Club Rd.

SELICA

Catheys Creek Church Rd.

64

Broad

Island Ford Rd.

French

River

P

P

1109   1110

Whitmire Rd.

US 64

Calvert Rd.

CALVERT

ROSMAN

Old Rosman Hwy

178

Walnut Hollow Road

Wolf
Gap

East Fork Road

20.2 Right on Island Ford Road (1110).
22.1 Left on South Country Club Road;
       end western loop (follow Bike
       Route 1/6).
23.8 Turn left on North Country
       Club Road.
23.9 Left on Illahee Road (1114); eastern
       loop (outbound Bike Route 1,
       right fork).
25.1 Left on four-lane US 64.
25.2 Right on Cashiers Valley Road
       (1344).
27.0 Left on Porbart Street (1348).
28.8 Right on North Oaklawn Avenue
       (1350); one block, left on North
       Main Street.
29.1 Cross US 64; one block,
       right on Gaston Street.

16. BREVARD TO ROSMAN

0   0.5   1mi
0   0.5   1km

N

© The Countryman Press

Brevard to Rosman

- **DISTANCE:** A 29.1-mile loop. The Short and Sweet version is a 7.6-mile loop. The Extra Credit ride is a 41-mile loop.
- **TERRAIN:** The ride follows rolling, low-traffic, paved back roads in the town of Brevard and in Transylvania County with one climb of 400 feet.
- **SPECIAL FEATURES:** Riding along the East Fork River and through the town of Brevard.
- **GENERAL LOCATION:** The ride connects the towns of Brevard and Rosman, North Carolina.
- **MAPS:** Transylvania County Bicycling is available from the North Carolina Department of Transportation.
- **ACCESS:** The ride starts in the center of Brevard. At the intersection of US 64 (Broad Street) and Main Street by the courthouse, turn on East Main Street. Turn left in one block on Gaston Street and park in the lot near the intersection with East Jordan Street.

Transylvania County has some of the most varied topography in the Blue Ridge. The county extends from the crest of the Blue Ridge, at elevations over 6,000 feet, to the Blue Ridge escarpment, where the mountains drop off to meet the piedmont below. All this elevation change, when combined with plenty of water from rain and snow, is a perfect recipe for waterfalls, which the county has in abundance—some 250 of them, by the official count.

The waterfalls and mountain scenery have made the Brevard area a longtime favorite of summer visitors. The hiking and fishing opportunities are almost limitless. Just outside of town are prime mountain biking areas along the North Mills and Davidson Rivers. The North Carolina Department of Transportation has also designated and marked eight bike routes through the county. The Brevard to Rosman ride uses two of these bike routes to explore Brevard, traverse the valley of the French Broad River, and follow the frolicking water of the East Fork River.

The ride is a barbell shape with an eastern loop through Brevard, a western loop out to Rosman, and a short connector in between. The ride follows Transylvania County Bike Route 1 outbound and returns on Bike Route 6. The routes use city streets in Brevard and scenic county roads in rural areas.

0.0 Begin by riding south on Gaston Street past South Broad Park.

0.4 At the end of Gaston Street, turn right and ride one block.

0.5 Turn left on South Broad Street, which is US 64.
Though not signed, this is part of Transylvania County Bike Route 1. Traffic on South Broad may be heavy, so riding the sidewalk is an option here.

0.7 Bear left on North Country Club Road where US 64 continues right.

1.3 The sidewalk ends at Brevard High School.
The road has little shoulder but is posted at 35 mph and sees less traffic here. Pass the Brevard Country Club.

2.4 Turn left at the intersection with Illahee Road and Bike Route 6.
For the next 1.9 miles, Bike Routes 1 and 6 will coincide along the connection between our ride's two loops.

2.6 Turn right on South Country Club Road (#1113).

4.3 Turn left at a T-junction on Island Farm Road (#1110) to follow Bike Route 1.
This intersection marks the start of the second loop of the ride. Bike Route 6 splits off to the right.

The scenic East Fork features many rapids and small waterfalls.

4.8 Cross the quiet flatwater of the French Broad River at Island Ford River Access.
The parking area here is an alternate starting point for the ride.

5.1 Turn right on Walnut Hollow Road (#1103).
Bike Route 4 begins on the left and leads 20.5 miles to Bike Route 8 east of Brevard.
   Begin a steady climb of 400 feet to Wolfs Gap.

6.8 From the hilltop enjoy an exhilarating drop back down to the floodplain of the French Broad River.

8.6 Turn right on East Fork Road (#1107).
The ride along the East Fork into Rosman is dotted with views of rapids and small waterfalls. The lovely stream is a favorite of anglers.

12.3 Turn right on Pickens Highway (US 178).
The unofficial Toxaway Connector Bike Route starts to the left.

13.1 After crossing the French Broad River, turn right on Main Street (#1156) at a stop sign in the heart of Rosman.
This is the end of Bike Route 1 and the start of Bike Route 6. Bike Route 5 also begins at the stop light and follows US 276 for 16.5 steep miles up to the Blue Ridge Parkway. Rosman has a gas station and convenience store if you need to refuel for the ride back to Brevard.

13.6 Turn right on Old Rosman Highway (#1388).

15.0 Turn right on Calvert Road (#1195).

16.1 Turn right on Whitmire Road by Mount Moriah Cherryfield Baptist Church.

17.7 Turn left on Little Egypt (#1185) and ride through the subdivision of the same name.

18.2 Turn left on Garland Road (#1190).
In about 100 yards the road crosses US 64. Use caution getting across this high-speed road.

18.3 Turn right at a T-junction on Catheys Creek Church Road (#1394).

19.4 Cross US 64 on Knox Crossing (#1159).
Bike Route 6 officially follows US 64E along the shoulder of this four-lane highway. By taking Knox Crossing a block south, then turning left on Old County Home Road, you can eliminate 0.4 mile of highway riding.

19.8 Turn left on Field Crossing, which intersects US 64 in one block, and then turn right and ride the shoulder of US 64.

20.2 Turn right on Island Ford Road (#1110).
Enjoy a pretty ride down to the floodplain of the French Broad River.

22.1 Turn left on South Country Club Road to close the western loop of the ride.
For the next 1.9 miles, the ride follows the combined Bike Routes 1 and 6.

23.8 Turn left on North Country Club Road.

23.9 Turn left on Illahee Road (#1114) and enter the eastern loop with a climb up a small hill.
Your outbound route on Bike Route 1 is the right fork.

25.1 Turn left on US 64, which is a four-lane highway with a narrow shoulder. *Be very careful both crossing the highway and riding along it.*

25.2 Turn right on Cashiers Valley Road (#1344) and ride through a residential area.

27.0 Turn left on Porbart Street (#1348) and ride past the Brevard Music Center and into Brevard.

28.8 Turn right on North Oaklawn Avenue (#1350).
In one block turn left on North Main Street and ride through Brevard's downtown area. There are public rest rooms and a water fountain in the City of Brevard Building.

29.1 Cross US 64 in the center of Brevard.
In one block turn right on Gaston Street to reach the parking area.

Short and Sweet: You can ride either the east loop through Brevard for 7.6 miles or the west loop through Rosman for 17.8 miles. For the west loop, use the parking area at Island Ford River Access.

For Extra Credit: Extend your ride 12 miles west on the Toxaway Connector Bike Route with a loop around Old Toxaway (#1139) and Frozen Creek (#1143) Roads, plus a short stretch of US 64.

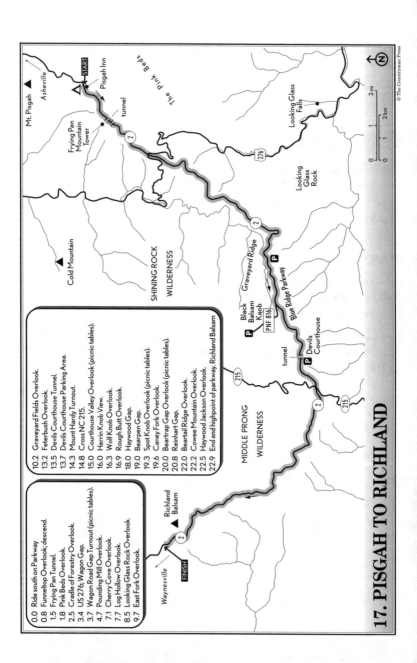

17. PISGAH TO RICHLAND

0.0   Ride south on Parkway
0.8   Funneltop Overlook; descend.
1.5   Frying Pan Tunnel.
1.8   Pink Beds Overlook.
2.5   Cradle of Forestry Overlook.
3.4   US 276; Wagon Gap.
3.7   Wagon Road Gap Turnout (picnic tables).
4.7   Pounding Mill Overlook.
7.1   Cherry Cove Overlook.
7.7   Log Hollow Overlook.
8.5   Looking Glass Rock Overlook.
9.7   East Fork Overlook.

10.2 Graveyard Fields Overlook.
13.2 Feterbush Overlook.
13.5 Devils Courthouse Tunnel.
13.7 Devils Courthouse Parking Area.
14.3 Mount Hardy Turnout.
14.8 Cross NC 215.
15.0 Courthouse Valley Overlook (picnic tables).
16.0 Herrin Knob View.
16.3 Wolf Knob Overlook.
16.9 Rough Butt Overlook.
18.0 Haywood Gap.
19.0 Bearpen Gap.
19.3 Spot Knob Overlook (picnic tables).
19.6 Caney Fork Overlook.
20.0 Beartrap Gap Overlook (picnic tables).
20.8 Reinhart Gap.
22.0 Beartail Ridge Overlook.
22.2 Cowee Mountain Overlook.
22.5 Haywood Jackson Overlook.
22.9 End and highpoint of parkway, Richland Balsam

© The Countryman Press

17

Pisgah to Richland

- **DISTANCE:** 22.9 miles one way. The Short and Sweet version is 7.9 miles one way. The Extra Credit ride is 45.8 miles round trip.
- **TERRAIN:** This section of the Blue Ridge Parkway is a hilly mountain road and contains climbs of 1,100 feet and 600 feet.
- **SPECIAL FEATURES:** Spectacular scenery and a climb to Richland Balsam, the highest point on the Blue Ridge Parkway.
- **GENERAL LOCATION:** The ride starts 20 miles southwest of Asheville, North Carolina, at Mount Pisgah.
- **MAPS:** Blue Ridge Parkway Official Map and Guide.
- **ACCESS:** From Asheville (near milepost 394), drive south on the Blue Ridge Parkway to Richland Balsam (milepost 431.4) to leave a vehicle for the return. Drive north back to the Pisgah Inn (milepost 408.5) to start the ride. To reach Richland Balsam from the south at the intersection with US 23/74, drive north on the parkway for 12.3 miles.

Just south of Asheville, North Carolina, is one of the Blue Ridge Parkway's most scenic sections. Here the road hugs the crest of the Great Balsam Range, home to 6,000-foot peaks and two popular Wilderness Areas. Riders will also enjoy some of the parkway's most famous and breathtaking vistas as they gaze upon Yellowstone Falls, Devils Courthouse, and Cold Mountain.

Riding the Blue Ridge Parkway near Pounding Mill Overlook

On the slopes of Richland Balsam, the parkway reaches its highest point at 6,053 feet. To avoid the punishing climbs needed to reach the high country from either Asheville or US 23/74, this section starts at the 5,000-foot-high Pisgah Inn and traverses the heart of this mountain oasis. There are two tunnels along the route. The shorter one (Frying Pan Tunnel) is easy to pass through; however, be careful to make sure you have time to get all the way through the longer Devils Courthouse Tunnel without encountering auto traffic. Lights and reflectors are very helpful in the tunnels along the parkway.

Though there are no services along this stretch of the parkway, the Mount Pisgah Area has most things a traveler needs including a lodge, a store, a gas station, a campground, a picnic area, and best of all, a restaurant for replenishing those carbos burned up along the road. Most facilities along the parkway close for the season around the end of October.

0.0 From the parking area at the Pisgah Inn, turn left and follow the parkway south.
This entire ride is part of North Carolina Bike Route 2, the Mountains-to-Sea Bike Route.

0.1 Pass the entrance to Pisgah Campground. There are 140 sites at this popular area.
The fire tower on Fryingpan Mountain is visible ahead.

0.8 Pass Funneltop Overlook (4,925 feet) on the left and begin a gentle descent.

1.5 Enter Fryingpan Tunnel.
Make sure no traffic is approaching when you enter this short, straight tunnel.

1.8 Pass Pink Beds Overlook (4,822 feet).
The pink beds are named for the dense groves of Catawba rhododendron and the color of their early summer blooms.

2.5 Pass Cradle of Forestry Overlook (4,710 feet) and MP 411.

3.4 Cross US 276 at Wagon Gap (4,535 feet).
North Carolina Bike Route 8 starts at the junction of the parkway and US 276.

The route (also called the Southern Highlands Route) goes south along US 276 to Brevard and ends in approximately 118 miles near Lincolnton. Bike Route 2 (North Carolina's Mountains-to-Sea Bike Route) continues south on the parkway. The trail extends for 700 miles from the mountains in Murphy to the Atlantic Ocean near Manteo. From Balsam Gap at US 23/74 to NC 181 near Linville, Bike Route 2 follows the Blue Ridge Parkway.

3.7 Pass Wagon Road Gap Turnout (4,550 feet) on the left. There are picnic tables and a trailhead for the Mountains-to-Sea Trail.

4.0 Reach Pigeon Gap (4,520 feet) and begin climbing.
Your slow pace will allow you to scan the roadside for wildflowers. Even in the heat of midsummer, fire pink and spiderwort will be in bloom.

4.7 Pass Pounding Mill Overlook (4,700 feet).
Descend and pass two more crossings of the Mountains-to-Sea Trail.

7.1 Pass Cherry Cove Overlook (4,327 feet) on the left and begin climbing.

7.7 Pass Log Hollow Overlook (4,445 feet) on the left.

8.5 Pass Looking Glass Rock Overlook (4,492 feet) and a Mountains-to-Sea Trailhead.
Looking Glass Rock is the centerpiece of a spectacular recreation area located between Brevard, North Carolina, and the Blue Ridge Parkway. The nearby Davidson River is renown for beautiful, but rugged, mountain biking. There is also a dense web of hiking trails, including the route to the top of Looking Glass Rock. The rock itself is a smooth dome of polished granite, sculpted from the softer rocks surrounding it through millions of years of erosion. Nearby John Rock and Cedar Rock Mountain are also part of a belt of these domes that lie along the eastern edge of the Blue Ridge escarpment. If you have ridden the parkway between Cumberland Knob and Doughton Park, Looking Glass Rock will remind you of Stone Mountain.

   Begin climbing. In the next 3.3 miles the road gains 1,100 feet.

9.7 Pass East Fork Overlook (4,995 feet) on the right.
Since crossing US 276, most of the land to the north of the parkway has been part of Shining Rock Wilderness. Shining Rock and the adjacent Middle Prong Wilderness combine to form one of the largest and most popular official wilderness areas in the Southern Appalachians. From this overlook the heart of the wilderness

is in view. The crest of the Great Balsams can be seen from Black Balsam Knob at the south end to Cold Mountain, now made famous by Charles Frazier's best-selling novel, at the north end.

10.2 Pass Graveyard Fields Overlook on the right and the trailhead for Yellowstone Falls.
Graveyard Fields got its name from the litter of dead trees that once filled this small valley, but the scenery has improved greatly since that time. The views include the Great Balsams; and the two waterfalls on the East Fork of the Pigeon River draw enough visitors to fill the large parking area on summer weekends.

10.8 Pass a short side road leading left to a hilltop picnic area.

11.6 Pass Pisgah National Forest Road 816 leading right.
This road leads 0.8 mile to the popular trailhead for the short walk to Black Balsam Knob and the longer trails heading north toward Shining Rock Gap. Just beyond the road your climb from Looking Glass Rock Overlook ends.

12.7 Cross a spur of the Mountains-to-Sea Trail.

13.2 Pass Feterbush Overlook (5,494 feet).

13.5 Enter Devils Courthouse Tunnel.
This long tunnel has a slight curve that restricts vision. It is important to make sure no cars are coming before entering the tunnel, and it is important to get through the tunnel as fast as possible. Remember that you will be especially difficult for vehicles to see. Also, remember the habit of honking car horns in tunnels is age old, so don't be startled if a driver blasts his horn in passing.

13.7 Pass Devils Courthouse Parking Area (5,720 feet) and a trailhead.
The courthouse is a massive rock outcrop offering magnificent views down into the Davidson River Valley. The popular hiking trail to the overlook is a 20-minute walk that begins at the north end of the parking area.

14.3 Pass Mount Hardy Turnout (5,415 feet).

14.8 Cross NC 215.
NC 215 leads south to Brevard, North Carolina, and north to Waynesville, North Carolina. North of the parkway it divides Middle Prong Wilderness and Shining Rock Wilderness. Transylvania County Bike Route 5 follows NC 215 for 16.5 miles

south to Rosman, while North Carolina Bike Route 2 continues south along the parkway.

15.0 Pass Courthouse Valley Overlook (5,362 feet), which has picnic tables.

16.0 Pass Herrin Knob View (5,510 feet) on the left.

16.3 Pass Wolf Knob Overlook (5,500 feet) on the left.

16.9 Pass Rough Butt Overlook (5,300 feet) on the left.

18.0 Cross Haywood Gap at 5,255 feet.
This is a trailhead for the Mountains-to-Sea Trail and the Middle Prong Wilderness. Begin a 400-foot climb.

19.0 Pass Bearpen Gap (5,560 feet) on the left.
This is also a trailhead for the Mountains-to-Sea Trail.

19.3 Pass Spot Knob Overlook with picnic tables.

19.6 Pass Caney Fork Overlook (5,650 feet) and milepost 428.
This is the end of the climb from Haywood Gap.

20.0 Pass Beartrap Gap Overlook (5,580 feet) with picnic tables.

20.8 Cross Reinhart Gap (5,455 feet) and pass milepost 429.
Begin the final 600-foot climb to Richland Balsam.

22.0 Pass Beartail Ridge Overlook (5,892 feet) on the left.

22.2 Pass Cowee Mountain Overlook on the left.
The vista here extends south across the rugged jumbled mountains of the Nantahala National Forest. The Cowee and Yellow Creek Mountains are some of the steepest and least visited of the Southern Appalachians.

22.5 Pass Haywood Jackson Overlook (6,020 feet) and milepost 431.

22.9 Reach the end of the ride at the highpoint of the Blue Ridge Parkway (6,053 feet) on the slopes of Richland Balsam.
Enjoy the fruits of your climb at a highpoint that even drivers and motorcyclists are grateful to reach. Only at Mount Mitchell in North Carolina and at Mount Washington in New Hampshire can you reach a higher point by road in the eastern half of the country. If you have any energy left, a 1.5-mile hiking trail leads through the red spruce and Fraser fir forest to the top of Richland Balsam at 6,410 feet.

Short and Sweet: To avoid the biggest climbs, start your ride at Devils Courthouse and enjoy a 7.9-mile ride to Richland Balsam.

For Extra Credit: Do a round trip for a total of 45.8 miles. If you start farther south from Asheville, add 14.8 miles one way and 3,700 feet of elevation gain. If you end farther north at US 23/74, add 12.3 miles one way and 2,500 feet of climbing.

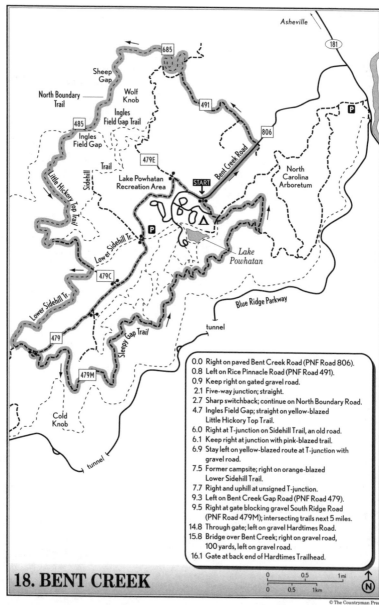

Asheville

181

685

Sheep
Gap

North Boundary
Trail

Wolf Knob

Ingles
Field Gap Trail

491

806

485

Ingles
Field Gap

479E

Bent Creek Road

Trail

START

North
Carolina
Arboretum

Sidehill

Lake Powhatan
Recreation Area

P

Little Hickory Top Trail

Δ

P

Lower Sidehill Tr.

Lake
Powhatan

479C

Lower Sidehill Tr.

Blue Ridge Parkway

479

Sleepy Gap Trail

tunnel

479M

Cold
Knob

tunnel

0.0 Right on paved Bent Creek Road (PNF Road 806).
0.8 Left on Rice Pinnacle Road (PNF Road 491).
0.9 Keep right on gated gravel road.
2.1 Five-way junction; straight.
2.7 Sharp switchback; continue on North Boundary Road.
4.7 Ingles Field Gap; straight on yellow-blazed
    Little Hickory Top Trail.
6.0 Right at T-junction on Sidehill Trail, an old road.
6.1 Keep right at junction with pink-blazed trail.
6.9 Stay left on yellow-blazed route at T-junction with
    gravel road.
7.5 Former campsite; right on orange-blazed
    Lower Sidehill Trail.
7.7 Right and uphill at unsigned T-junction.
9.3 Left on Bent Creek Gap Road (PNF Road 479).
9.5 Right at gate blocking gravel South Ridge Road
    (PNF Road 479M); intersecting trails next 5 miles.
14.8 Through gate; left on gravel Hardtimes Road.
15.8 Bridge over Bent Creek; right on gravel road,
    100 yards, left on gravel road.
16.1 Gate at back end of Hardtimes Trailhead.

18. BENT CREEK

| 0 | 0.5 | 1mi |
| 0 | 0.5 | 1km |

N

© The Countryman Press

Bent Creek

- **DISTANCE:** A 16.1-mile loop. The Short and Sweet version is a 9.8-mile loop. The Extra Credit ride is a 16.6-mile loop.

- **TERRAIN:** Mostly closed gravel roads with some open gravel roads and singletrack trails. The loop includes 1,000 feet of climbing and some short rocky sections.

- **SPECIAL FEATURES:** The ride is an introduction to one of the finest mountain biking areas in the Southeast.

- **GENERAL LOCATION:** 4 miles from I-26 near Asheville, North Carolina.

- **MAPS:** Trails Illustrated Pisgah Ranger District, North Carolina #780. A more detailed set of maps can be found on www.mtbike wnc.com.

- **ACCESS:** Take Exit 2 from I-26 just south of Asheville. Drive 2 miles south on NC 191, then turn right on Bent Creek Road at signs for Lake Powatan Recreation Area. Drive 2.2 miles to the Hardtimes Trailhead and park.

Nirvana on the edge of town. Few communities have recreational opportunities right outside the back door that compare to Asheville, North Carolina, a bipolar bastion of retirees and expatriated hippies whose unofficial motto is "Where old age meets new age." Asheville's nearby hiking trails, bike routes, and whitewater runs have long made it a mecca for outdoor lovers. Of all the great places lurking on the outskirts of town, perhaps the Bent Creek Experimental Forest is the most remarkable.

Bent Creek is a great place to observe the Forest Service's efforts to provide a "Land of Many Uses." First of all, Bent Creek is a research forest, a legacy that stretches back to the first efforts to apply the European science of forestry in America. George Vanderbilt, heir to an immense railroad fortune and builder of the Biltmore Estate, once owned nearly all of what is now the Pisgah Ranger District. With remarkable foresight, he hired pioneer foresters Gifford Pinchot and Carl Schenck to manage his lands. Adjacent to Bent Creek is the North Carolina Arboretum, which is managed through North Carolina State University.

At the heart of Bent Creek is Lake Powatan Recreation Area. The area features a large campground, a small lake, and a network of trails loved by hikers, horseback riders, hunters, and

Approaching Five Points on singletrack trail at Bent Creek

mountain bikers. In May of 2002, the Forest Service approved a new plan to manage the area. Key to the new plan is better management of the trail system. The new plan designates 47 miles of trails—23 miles are open to mountain bikers and 18 miles will be open to horseback riders. New loop trails will be established from South Ridge Road to Explorer Loop and from Ledford Branch Road to Fern Branch Trail. An additional 17 miles of gated roads will also be open to mountain bikers and horseback riders. Other non-system trails, many of which are unofficial singletrack, will be closed to reduce impacts on the research forest.

Other management changes are in the works as well. Camping has already been restricted to the official sites at Lake Powatan Campground. Better parking facilities will be built at Rice Pinnacle Road, Boyd Branch Road, South Ridge Road, and Long Branch. Finally, some of the seasonal trail closures for mountain bikers and horseback riders will be lifted during hunting season. Check with the Pisgah Ranger District for the latest trail conditions and information.

The changes coming to Bent Creek are the result of compromises between the various users of the land. Compromises by their nature never leave any group totally satisfied, but mountain bikers have won a lot with this plan. The main mountain biking trails at Bent Creek are still intact, and Forest Service designation of more of these trails should lead to better signing and upkeep. In its current state, Bent Creek can be an intimidating system for the first-time rider. There are a number of unofficial side trails, and many junctions are not signed. The Pisgah National Forest plans a logging operation in the experimental forest for sometime after 2003 that may affect some of the trails at Bent Creek. The timber operation will have a short-term impact on mountain biking as some roads may be closed while they are used for timber removal. Check with the Pisgah Ranger District, the Supervisors Office, or the information stations at Bent Creek for further information on this project.

This perimeter ride is a good introduction to Bent Creek. Most of the route is gated two-track gravel road. Some of these old roads have narrowed to singletrack, but even these trails have only a few, short rough stretches. Since many of the currently existing single-track trails will be eliminated under the Pisgah National Forest's new plan, not every possible junction will be described below.

0.0 From the trailhead turn right on the paved Bent Creek Road, which is Pisgah National Forest (PNF) Road 806.

0.8 Turn left on Rice Pinnacle Road (PNF Road 491).

0.9 Keep right on a gated gravel road with parking on the left.
The Forest Service plans to develop a new trailhead here. Next pass a house with a sculpture of flying biker in front.

1.1 Pass the gated, gravel PNF Road 491A on the left.
Pass several singletrack trails on the left, including one at the site of a stand that was clear-cut in 1967.

2.1 Go straight through a five-way junction where the auto tour route follows a gravel road to the left and singletrack trails lead right and from the far left corner. Pass several other switchbacks and one old road leading right.

2.7 At a sharp switchback, a singletrack trail leads left.
North Boundary Road now begins to narrow and starts a steadier climb up the northern limit of the Bent Creek watershed. In midsummer parts of the trail to Ingles Field Gap narrow to singletrack and can become brushy.

4.2 Begin a downhill ride to Ingles Field Gap.

4.7 Reach Ingles Field Gap, which is also called 5 Points or the Top.
Here North Boundary Road continues ahead to the right along the ridgetop, a faint singletrack leads sharply right, and Ingles Field Gap Trail leads left steeply down to Sidehill Trail. Our route continues straight on the signed Little Hickory Top Trail, which is marked with yellow blazes. The descent from Ingles Field Gap to Lower Sidehill Trail is the roughest riding of the loop. Little Hickory Top is a rolling singletrack with some rocks and two short, steep chutes where some riders may want to walk their bikes.

6.0 Turn right at a T-junction on Sidehill Trail, which is an old road.

6.1 Keep right at a junction with a pink-blazed shortcut trail.
Watch for some rocky switchbacks just after you cross a small creek.

6.8 Cross a larger stream and reach another sign for Sidehill Trail. The pink-blazed shortcut trail enters from the left along the stream.

6.9 Stay left on the yellow-blazed route at a T-junction with a gravel road. *The road will soon widen at a SIDEHILL TRAIL sign where a singletrack trail leads left. The downhill beyond is smooth, fast, and fun.*

7.5 At a former campsite, turn right on the orange-blazed Lower Sidehill Trail, which is a singletrack closed to horseback riders.

7.7 Turn right and uphill at an unsigned T-junction in a grove of hemlocks. *This climb is steep and rocky in places.*

8.4 At the top of the grade, the trail becomes a smooth, fun ride. *There is, however, one last rocky section just before reaching Bent Creek Gap Road.*

9.3 Go left on the well-maintained Bent Creek Gap Road (PNF Road 479).

9.5 Turn right at a gate blocking the gravel South Ridge Road (PNF Road 479M). *The rest of the ride is now on wide, closed gravel roads. The road begins with a gentle climb.*

10.7 Pass an intersection with the signed and red-blazed Chestnut Cove Trail.

12.4 Cross the signed and red-blazed Sleepy Gap Trail. *This trail is currently closed to mountain bikers between April and October.*

13.0 Cross another spur of Sleepy Gap Trail.

13.8 Cross the signed Deerfield Trail, which is open to foot travel only.

14.8 Turn left on the gravel Hardtimes Road after passing through a gate. *Enjoy a fun, fast downhill ride.*

15.8 Reach the concrete bridge over Bent Creek and a T-junction with another gravel road leading right to the North Carolina Arboretum and left to Lake Powatan. *A hiking trail crosses at the bridge. Turn right on the gravel road, and in about 100 yards, turn left on a gravel road marked by a post.*

16.1 After passing several side trails, the gravel road reaches the gate at the back end of the Hardtimes Trailhead.

Short and Sweet: For a ride that is all gravel road with a minimum of climbing and traffic, head out on Bent Creek Gap Road (PNF Road 479) to join the perimeter ride at 9.5 miles. You'll return on South Ridge Road (PNF Road 479M) for a 9.8-mile loop.

For Extra Credit: One way to extend the mileage of this loop is to use North Boundary Road instead of Little Hickory Top Trail, adding about 0.5 mile. More advanced riders will want to up their singletrack experience by riding Fern Glen and Sidehill Trails to Ingles Field Gap, which is the same distance as PNF Road 491 and North Boundary Road. Or, by continuing on PNF Road 479 to Bent Creek Gap, riders can access the extensive system of trails south of the Blue Ridge Parkway along the North Fork of Mills River.

19

All Around Asheville

- **DISTANCE:** A 24.5-mile loop. The Short and Sweet version is 7.8 miles round trip. The Extra Credit ride is a 26.4-mile loop.
- **TERRAIN:** An intricate circle around the city on paved roads with climbs of 400 feet and 300 feet.
- **SPECIAL FEATURES:** Hilltop views of Asheville, beautiful neighborhoods, and the Grove Park Inn.
- **GENERAL LOCATION:** The ride links the town of Biltmore Forest with the City of Asheville.
- **MAPS:** Bicycle Transportation Map Asheville and Buncombe County North Carolina is available from the City of Asheville.
- **ACCESS:** There is a small turnout just east of the Hendersonville Road Exit from the Blue Ridge Parkway near milepost 389. An alternative starting point is at Jean Webb Park on Riverside Drive.

Asheville, North Carolina, is perhaps the region's most bicycle friendly city. City planners have produced a handy map for cyclists that rates city and county roads by the volume and speed of traffic. The map is the key to the kingdom for those looking to explore the city on two wheels. The city has also marked 10 short neighborhood loop rides; you will encounter several of them on this loop.

This ride begins in the town of Biltmore Forest, a wealthy community that borders the Biltmore Estate, the colossal mansion and

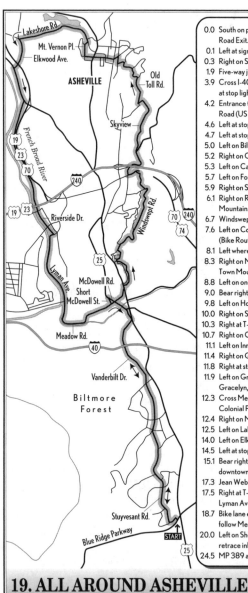

0.0 South on parkway toward Hendersonville Road Exit.

0.1 Left at sign for Biltmore Forest.

0.3 Right on Stuyvesant Road.

1.9 Five-way junction; straight on Vanderbilt Road.

3.9 Cross I-40, left on Hendersonville Road (US 25) at stop light.

4.2 Entrance to Biltmore; bear left to follow McDowell Road (US 25).

4.6 Left at stop light down Short McDowell Street.

4.7 Left at stop light on Meadow Road.

5.0 Left on Biltmore Avenue.

5.2 Right on Caledonia Road.

5.3 Left on Castle Street; climb.

5.7 Left on Forest Hill.

5.9 Right on Sherwood; Bike Route 7 uphill.

6.1 Right on Reservoir Road; climb Beaucatcher Mountain.

6.7 Windswept Drive along ridgecrest.

7.6 Left on College Street at T-junction (Bike Route 7, right).

8.1 Left where College Street follows US 70/74.

8.3 Right on Martin Luther King Boulevard; becomes Town Mountain Road (NC 694).

8.8 Left on one-way Skyview Place.

9.0 Bear right on Sunset Drive.

9.8 Left on Howland Road; Bike Route 3.

10.0 Right on Sunset Trail; downhill.

10.3 Right at T-junction on Macon Avenue.

10.7 Right on Old Toll Road; Grove Park Inn.

11.1 Left on Innsbruck Road.

11.4 Right on Grovewood Road at stop sign.

11.8 Right at stop sign on Country Club Road.

11.9 Left on Griffing Boulevard at stop sign; becomes Gracelyn, joins Bike Route 8.

12.3 Cross Merrimon Avenue (US 25); becomes Colonial Place.

12.4 Right on Mount Vernon Place.

12.5 Left on Lakeshore Road.

14.0 Left on Elkwood Avenue; under US 19/23/70.

14.5 Left at stop light on Riverside Drive.

15.1 Bear right; Broadway Street heads left toward downtown.

17.3 Jean Webb River Park.

17.5 Right at T-junction; left at stop sign on Lyman Avenue.

18.7 Bike lane ends near Carrier Bridge; straight to follow Meadow Road.

20.0 Left on Short McDowell Street at end of loop; retrace inbound route to parkway.

24.5 MP 389 and Hendersonville Road Exit.

19. ALL AROUND ASHEVILLE

0   0.5   1mi
0   0.5   1km

grounds built by the Vanderbilt family. After passing the entrance of the Biltmore Estate, the ride begins a loop by climbing two high ridges for views of downtown Asheville before descending to the entrance of the famed Grove Park Inn. The route then passes by Beaver Lake before paralleling the French Broad River through one of the city's industrial areas. After closing the loop, the ride returns to the Blue Ridge Parkway by retracing the route through Biltmore Forest.

Stitching together all these features requires a somewhat intricate route. You'll need to pay attention to the route and your map for the first 12.5 miles to Lakeshore Road and then you can open up the bike and get some exercise.

This ride uses city streets, some of which can occasionally carry heavy traffic. In general, the roads here have little traffic, reasonable speeds, and drivers accustomed to cyclists. However, this is not always the case, and therefore, this ride is not suited for beginners or children.

0.0 Ride south on the parkway toward the Hendersonville Road Exit.

0.1 From the exit, turn left at a sign for Biltmore Forest.

0.3 Make a right turn on Stuyvesant Road.
The town of Biltmore Forest contains some of the finest homes in the Asheville area. Though not quite as elaborate as the Biltmore Estate, the neighborhood looks like the type where even the servants have help.

1.9 Go straight at a five-way junction on Vanderbilt Road.

3.9 After crossing over I-40, turn left on Hendersonville Road (US 25) at a stop light and head toward the entrance of the Biltmore Estate.
Traffic on Hendersonville Road may be heavy, so try riding the sidewalk or cutting through parking lots on this short stretch.

4.2 At the entrance to the Biltmore Estate, bear left to follow McDowell Road (US 25) across a bridge over the Swannanoa River.
The Biltmore Estate was constructed between 1889 and 1895 for George Vanderbilt, heir to the family railroad fortune. The estate is a monument to an age of opulence that those who inflated the internet bubble could only have dreamed

of. At one time the Biltmore Estate was America's largest private home; now it is a business enterprise in its own right. The mansion contains 250 rooms (imagine trying to find your lost car keys in that house). Though it contains features such as electricity, central heat, and refrigeration, which were state of the art at the time, the family couldn't get by with less than 65 fireplaces. The 8,000-acre estate is open to tourists who pay a fee for tours of the house, gardens, and on-site winery. The Biltmore Estate also offers hiking, biking, river trips, and horseback riding.

4.6 Turn left at a stop light and head down Short McDowell Street.

4.7 Turn left at a stop light on Meadow Road.
Meadow Road marks the start of the loop portion of the ride.

5.0 Turn left on Biltmore Avenue.
This is the continuation of Hendersonville Road and may have heavy traffic. However, there is a sidewalk for this short stretch.

5.2 Turn right on Caledonia Road.

5.3 Turn left on Castle Street and climb steeply.

5.7 Turn left on Forest Hill Drive.

5.9 Turn right on Sherwood Road and begin following Asheville Bike Route 7 uphill.

6.1 Turn right on Reservoir Road and begin a steep climb up Beaucatcher Mountain.
Beaucatcher Mountain is the prominent ridge on the east side of Asheville.

6.7 Follow Windswept Drive along the ridgecrest.
On clear days, the views down to the center of Asheville are spectacular. This is a good spot to test your brakes for the steep winding descent to come.

7.6 Turn left on College Street at a T-junction where Bike Route 7 goes right.
The descent is still steep and has one switchback.

8.1 Turn left where College Street follows US 70/74.
You can use the sidewalk here.

8.3 Turn right on Martin Luther King Boulevard, which becomes Town Mountain Road (NC 694).
Begin a steep climb with more views of downtown Asheville.

Entrance to the Biltmore Estate

8.8 Turn left to follow one-way Skyview Place.

9.0 Bear right on Sunset Drive.
Here is another pedestrian-friendly neighborhood with especially interesting architecture.

9.8 Turn left on Howland Road and begin following Bike Route 3.

10.0 Turn right on Sunset Trail and ride down a steep hill with switchbacks.

10.3 Go right at a T-junction on Macon Avenue.

10.7 Go right on Old Toll Road at the entrance to the Grove Park Inn.
A small observation platform near the entrance is a handy vantage point for photographing one of America's most prestigious resorts. Construction of the handsome stone building was started in 1912 and included stone blocks as large as five tons. The 140-acre grounds include a private golf course. The inn marks the start of a gentle climb.

11.1 Turn left on Innsbruck Road.

11.4 Turn right on Grovewood Road at a stop sign.

11.8 Turn right at a stop sign on Country Club Road.

11.9 Turn left on Griffing Boulevard at a stop sign.
At the intersection with Kimberly Avenue, the road is renamed Gracelyn Road and later joins Asheville Bike Route 8.

12.3 Cross Merrimon Avenue (US 25) where there are fast-road restaurants and the road is renamed Colonial Place.

12.4 Turn right on Mount Vernon Place.

12.5 Turn left on Lakeshore Road.
Up to this point the ride has been hilly and intricate, requiring careful attention to both map and traffic. This is about to change. From here on the riding is flat, fast, and relatively straightforward.

14.0 Turn left on Elkwood Avenue and ride under US 19/23/70 to the French Broad River.

14.5 Turn left at a stop light on Riverside Drive.
Riverside Drive is used by several of Asheville's bike routes.

15.1 Bear right where Broadway Street heads left toward downtown.
Riverside Drive provides access to an industrial section of Asheville. There is ample shoulder for riding on most of the road and a 1.2-mile bike lane along the rest.

17.3 Pass Jean Webb River Park and Picnic Area.
The gravel parking area here provides an alternate starting point for the ride.

17.5 Turn right at a T-junction, then left at a stop sign on Lyman Avenue.
This is a prettier riverside ride with a bike lane. On the far bank is the French Broad River Park.

18.7 The bike lane ends near Carrier Bridge. Keep straight to follow Meadow Road.

20.0 Turn left on Short McDowell Street at the end of the loop.
Retrace your inbound route back to the Blue Ridge Parkway.

24.5 End at the parkway near milepost 389 and the Hendersonville Road off-ramp.

Short and Sweet: Ride the Biltmore Forest leg for a 7.8-mile round trip.

For Extra Credit: From Lakeshore Road, ride Elk Mountain Road to Riverside Drive for an extra 1.9 miles.

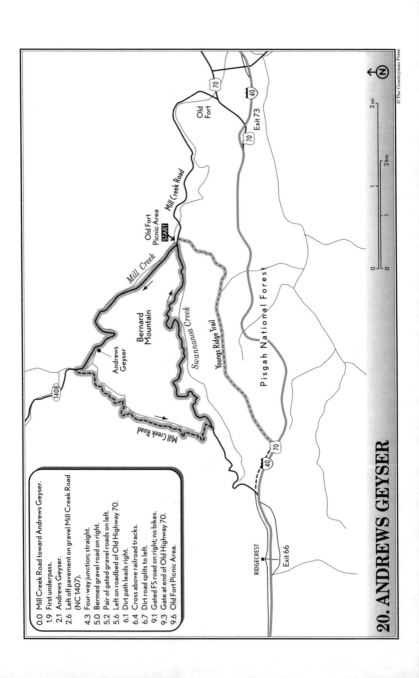

0.0 Mill Creek Road toward Andrews Geyser.
1.9 First underpass.
2.1 Andrews Geyser.
2.6 Left off pavement on gravel Mill Creek Road (NC 1407).
4.3 Four-way junction; straight.
5.0 Bermed gravel road on right.
5.2 Pair of gated gravel roads on left.
5.6 Left on roadbed of Old Highway 70.
6.1 Dirt path leads right.
6.4 Cross above railroad tracks.
6.7 Dirt road splits to left.
9.1 Gated FS road on right; no bikes.
9.3 Gate at end of Old Highway 70.
9.6 Old Fort Picnic Area.

20. ANDREWS GEYSER

© The Countryman Press

Andrews Geyser

- **DISTANCE:** A 9.6-mile loop. The Short and Sweet version is 6.1 miles one way. The Extra Credit ride is a steeper 9.2-mile loop.

- **TERRAIN:** The loop uses a combination of paved and well-maintained gravel roads, partly through the Grandfather Ranger District of the Pisgah National Forest. It includes an 800-foot climb from Andrews Geyser.

- **SPECIAL FEATURES:** Andrews Geyser and the descent along abandoned Old US 70.

- **GENERAL LOCATION:** About 3 miles west of Old Fort, North Carolina.

- **MAPS:** USGS Montreat and Old Fort, North Carolina quad-rangles.

- **ACCESS:** From Exit 73 off I-40 in Old Fort, turn north on Catawba Avenue and drive through downtown Old Fort. In 0.4 mile, turn left on US 70. At 0.7 mile, turn right on Old US 70, which is also Mill Creek Road and NC 1407. Reach the turnoff for Pisgah National Forest's Old Fort Picnic Area at 3.3 miles and the junction where Old US 70 (now NC 1400) continues straight. Park in the lot for the picnic area. The picnic area closes for the winter on November 1st. An alternate parking site is at Andrews Geyser.

Most great bike rides have a single signature attraction that separates them from the merely good rides. This loop boasts

A kudzu-enshrouded section of Old US 70

Andrews Geyser and Old US 70, a pair of features each unique enough to draw riders in droves.

The town of Old Fort marks the site of one of the easiest transportation routes up the steep eastern escarpment of the Blue Ridge Mountains. In the 1870s, the Western North Carolina Railroad followed historic Indian trails through this region to reach Asheville, North Carolina, and later built a wagon road though Swannanoa Gap. The wagon road was replaced in 1925 by a paved road, which became US 70. In the early 1950s, that road was bypassed when a new four-lane US 70 was built in the corridor to the south where I-40 is now located. Though Old US 70 is still a public area, it is now closed to vehicles and allows only hikers, cyclists, and horseback riders.

It is hard to tell when Old US 70 was last maintained, but Mother Nature has clearly run amok since then. Most of the surface is still paved, but a myriad of layers of concrete, asphalt, and gravel are exposed through cracks and rubble. Other riders have kept the roadway clear of fallen trees, but the surrounding vegetation is slowly overwhelming the roadbed. In the full bloom of summer's growth, vegetation can narrow the roadway to the width of single rider. If you have never seen what kudzu can do to landscape, when allowed to grow unchecked, the tenacious growth of this aggressive invader may shock you.

The road's surface, bridges and even guardrails are still intact, but otherwise there is little sign of civilization. It seems strange to see no remains of homes or businesses. No one must have lived or worked along this route; it was just a means to get somewhere else. The lush forest around the road emphasizes a sense of abandonment. The natural world is trying hard to reclaim the road for its own. On a hot summer day, the ride can be a bit eerie, like a trip through the twilight zone. Look for it soon on the set of a science fiction movie.

The history of Andrews Geyser is also linked to the evolution of the area's transportation system. Andrews Geyser is actually a manmade feature, built in the 1870s alongside a railway hotel to honor the arrival of the railroad into Western North Carolina. It is connected by pipe to a lake high above, along the Mill Creek Road, and can be turned on and off by a valve. In 1911, Andrews Geyser was rebuilt and named for Colonel Alexander Andrews, a railroad engineer who became the first president of the Western North Carolina Railroad. A second rehabilitation, in 1976, refurbished the geyser to its present condition. The site is now a pleasant park with picnic facilities. Because water flow to the geyser is controlled at the lake, a gushing geyser isn't guaranteed.

0.0 From the picnic area entrance, take Mill Creek Road toward Andrews Geyser.
The start of this ride is a gentle uphill on a smoothly paved road.

1.9 Reach the first of several one-lane underpasses below the railroad tracks.
These underpasses are very narrow, so make sure you are clear of traffic before riding through them.

2.1 Reach Andrews Geyser.
The geyser is fed through a pipe from the bottom of a lake at the Mill Creek Inn, which is located farther along this route. It may not be flowing on your visit. The site is now a city park with picnic tables, benches, shade trees, and small parking area.

2.6 Turn left off the pavement on the gravel Mill Creek Road (NC 1407) where NC 1408 continues ahead.
The gravel road marks the start of the long steady climb up the Blue Ridge escarpment. You will gain 800 feet in the next 2.6 miles. Though your ride may seem a long haul, the railroad engines that pull up this grade need even more help. You'll pass underneath a serpentine nest of rail lines, designed to lessen the grade for the heavily laden trains. Near the start of the climb, you'll also pass the Mill Creek Inn and the lake that provides water to Andrews Geyser.

4.3 Continue straight at a four-way junction with a pair of gated gravel roads.
Pisgah National Forest (PNF) Road 432, or Bernard Road, leads left, and PNF Road 1186 (Parish Creek Road) leads right up toward the Old Mitchell Toll Road.

5.0 Pass a bermed gravel road on the right.

5.2 Pass a pair of gated gravel roads on the left.
These roads mark the crest of the hill and the highpoint of the climb. The riding is all downhill from here.

5.6 Turn left on the roadbed of Old US 70. The road ahead becomes paved and leads into Ridgecrest.

There is a pullout for parking at this intersection.

Old US 70 is now officially called NC 1400. It is blocked by gates at both ends and is no longer maintained. The land around the upper end of the road is privately owned, so stay on the roadbed to respect private property. The Pisgah National Forest surrounds the lower part of the road. Though the roadway is still paved, don't expect a perfectly smooth ride. The road surface is disintegrating, and there are enough potholes and divots to throw an unwary rider off the bike. This part of the ride seems like an abandoned film set. In addition to great atmosphere, it also offers some great views.

6.1 A dirt path leads right.

6.4 Cross above the railroad tracks.

6.7 A dirt road splits off to the left.

9.1 A gated forest service road on the right is open to horseback riders and hikers.

9.3 Reach the gate (beside a private residence) at the end of Old US 70.

9.6 Reach the end of the ride at the entrance for Old Fort Picnic Area.

Short and Sweet: Take the ride downhill from the top of Old US 70 to Andrews Geyser for a 6.1-mile ride. To reach the turnout parking at the upper end of Old US 70 from I-40, take Exit 66 at Ridgecrest. Go north of the interstate and turn right at 0.1 mile (stop sign) on Old US 70 (Ridgecrest Road). Drive another 0.6 mile, past Ridgecrest Conference Center and turn left at a stop sign on Yates Road (NC 2702). In another 1.2 miles, reach the gate and parking area at the upper end of the paved Old US 70 where the gravel Mill Creek Road joins on the left.

For Extra Credit: For some singletrack excitement, ride the 3.5-mile Youngs Ridge Trail (PNF Trail 206) and the 0.5-mile Kitsuma Peak Trail (PNF Trail 205), climbing 1,500 feet up and over Kitsuma Peak from the Ridgecrest Conference Center to Old Fort Picnic Area. Ride back up Old US 70 for a 9.2-mile loop. Though shorter, this loop is steeper and the trail riding is more technical.

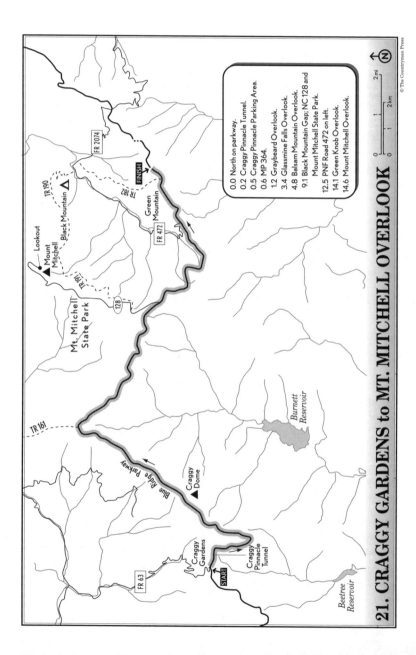

21. CRAGGY GARDENS to MT. MITCHELL OVERLOOK

0.0 North on parkway.
0.2 Craggy Pinnacle Tunnel.
0.5 Craggy Pinnacle Parking Area.
0.6 MP 364.
1.2 Graybeard Overlook.
3.4 Glassmine Falls Overlook.
4.8 Balsam Mountain Overlook.
9.1 Black Mountain Gap; NC 128 and
     Mount Mitchell State Park.
12.5 PNF Road 472 on left.
14.1 Green Knob Overlook.
14.6 Mount Mitchell Overlook.

N

0   1   2 mi
0   1   2 km

© The Countryman Press

21

Craggy Gardens to Mount Mitchell Overlook

- **DISTANCE:** 14.6 miles one way. The Short and Sweet version is 9.1 miles one way. The Extra Credit ride is 38.8 miles round trip.
- **TERRAIN:** The Blue Ridge Parkway is rarely flat, but the climbs are shorter than you might imagine.
- **SPECIAL FEATURES:** Spectacular vistas of the Black Mountains and the lush gardens around Craggy Pinnacle.
- **GENERAL LOCATION:** About 20 miles north of Asheville, North Carolina.
- **MAPS:** Blue Ridge Parkway Official Map and Guide.
- **ACCESS:** Enter the Blue Ridge Parkway on the east side of Asheville, North Carolina. About 18 miles beyond the Folk Art Center, park at the large lot for Craggy Gardens Visitor Center. To access the north end of the ride at Mount Mitchell Overlook, continue on the parkway to milepost 350, or drive south on the parkway from its junction with NC 80.

Craggy Gardens is best known for its early summer displays of rhododendron blossoms. The prolific blooms of the broad-leaved evergreen come in two colors: the rich purple of the higher elevation Catawba and the downy white of the lower elevation Rosebay. But these aren't the only flowers visitors are apt to find in bloom in early summer. Where rhododendron flourishes, you usually find its cousin the mountain laurel carpeting the forest floor with small white flowers. The less common orange buds of flame azalea are also easily found. These low-growing evergreens form dense mats on the mountaintops called heath balds, for their lack of tall trees. Blackberry, blueberry, and myrtle are also common in some heath balds.

On nearby Mount Mitchell, there's a sadder story about a much different evergreen. Here, the first outbreak was found in the Southern Appalachians of the balsam wooley adelgid in Fraser fir forests. The adelgid is a tiny parasite that feeds on the inner bark, eventually killing the tree. The ghost forests of dead firs on Mount Mitchell, and other prominent mountains such as Clingmans Dome in Great Smoky Mountains National Park, show how even tiny creatures can easily destroy the largest creatures, and can, in fact, change entire ecosystems.

But there is still hope for the Fraser fir. The adelgid can't enter the tree while the bark is still smooth, and luckily, the trees can reproduce before they grow large enough to force their bark to split. In addition, researchers have found small isolated stands of firs that seem impervious to the insect's attack. Whether there is something unique to the genetic makeup of these stands or there are other factors at work, scientists do not know. But perhaps these resistant strains will form the core of a new population, and the Fraser fir will avoid the fate of nearly extinct species such as the once mighty American chestnut.

This section of the Blue Ridge Parkway is one of the highest elevation sections along the entire 469-mile route. It is frequently closed in winter because of ice and snow. Craggy Gardens Visitor Center generally closes for the season around the end of October.

0.0 From the Visitor Center, turn left and ride north on the parkway.
This entire route is also part of the Mountains-to-Sea Bike Route (North Carolina Bike Route 2).

0.2 Take care entering the short Craggy Pinnacle Tunnel.

0.5 Pass Craggy Pinnacle Parking Area on the left.
The 0.7-mile walk to the summit of 5,892-foot Craggy Pinnacle is well worth the climb at any time of year for its fine views of the Blue Ridge, ranging from the

The Blue Ridge Parkway from the top of Craggy Dome

mountains south of Asheville to the Black Mountains. But you might want to save your energy until after the ride is over.

0.6 Pass milepost 364.

1.2 Pass Graybeard Overlook (5,365 feet) on the right.
Craggy Dome, immediately east of the overlook, is slightly higher than Craggy Pinnacle, but there is no trail to the top of the Dome. The land to the south of the parkway is part of the Asheville City watershed. Public use of the watershed is prohibited, and visitors are asked to stay within the parkway corridor. Descend steeply from the overlook. The Mountains-to-Sea Trail follows the narrow Blue Ridge Parkway corridor from Graybeard Overlook to Mount Mitchell State Park.

3.4 Pass Glassmine Falls Overlook (5,200 feet), which also offers access to the Mountains-to-Sea Trail.
The falls are visible on the steep slopes across from the overlook. The name is probably derived from the glassy reflection of water on the rocks rather than from any historical mining activity.

4.8 Pass Balsam Mountain Overlook (5,317 feet).
There is no view here; however, the parking area is used for the Mountains-to-Sea Trail, which crosses the parkway, and for access to Big Butt Trail. Begin climbing.

6.2 Crest a small hill and begin to descend.

9.1 Reach Black Mountain Gap (5,180 feet) where NC 128 joins the parkway.
This is the entrance road to Mount Mitchell State Park. North Carolina's first state park was created in 1915, partly in response to the fears over destructive logging practices that had nearly reached the mountain's highest slopes. The now 1,855 acre park protects the 6,000-foot-high mountain crest from Mount Gibbes to Cattail Peak. The park features a network of hiking trails, a restaurant open in season, a small campground, plus a lookout tower and museum on the mountaintop.
    NC 128 climbs steadily 4.8 miles to enter Mount Mitchell State Park and ends just below the tower atop the highest point in the eastern United States. This climb is the culmination of one of the Southeast's toughest organized road bike rides, the annual Assault on Mount Mitchell.

9.5 Reach the Bald Knob Ridge Trailhead at milepost 355.

9.8 Pass the gated, gravel Old Toll Road.
The area behind the gate is private property.

12.0 A turnout offers spectacular views of Mount Mitchell.

12.5 Pass the unsigned, gravel PNF Road 472 (4,283 feet) on the left leading to Pisgah National Forest's Mount Mitchell Campground and the valley of the South Toe River.

14.1 Pass Green Knob Overlook (4,760 feet).
The views northeast from here extend over Lake James and the towns of Morganton and Marion.

14.2 Pass the well-disguised trailhead on the left for Green Mountain Trail.
Though a little overgrown during summer at its start, this 1-mile, round-trip walk is more than just a great leg stretcher. There is a spacious lookout tower on top with views stretching all across the Black Range and north along the parkway to Crabtree Meadows. Just be sure to bear left at the unsigned fork in the trail; the right fork will lead down to the South Toe River Valley. If you want to enjoy all the views of Mount Mitchell Overlook without any cars whizzing by, this is the place to go. The trail's high elevation ensures that rhododendron blossoms stay late, and even in summer, some fire pinks and bluets may bloom beside the trail.

14.6 Reach the end of the ride at Mount Mitchell Overlook.
Here the views of the Black Range extend from the rocky shoulder of Potato Knob, north to the bristle of towers on top of Clingmans Peak, and then to the Crown of the East, the single lookout tower on top of Mount Mitchell. The string of 6,000-foot summits continues north from Mount Mitchell to its near neighbor Mount Craig and for another 6 miles to the end of the range at Cello Knob.

Short and Sweet: End your ride at NC 128 after 9.1 miles.

For Extra Credit: The ride is 29.2 miles round trip, or you can add an extra 9.6 miles and 1,400 feet of climbing by riding to the Mount Mitchell summit parking area.

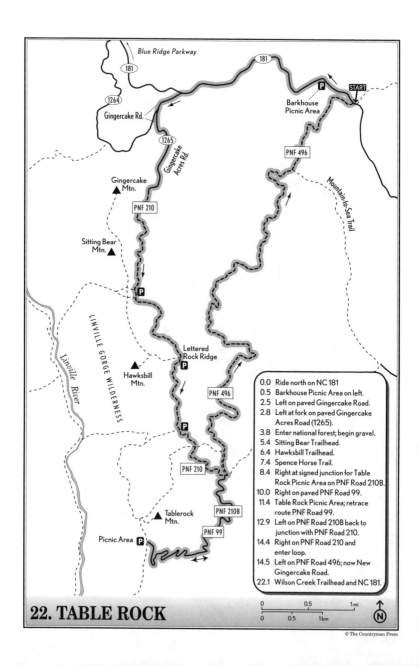

Blue Ridge Parkway

181

1264

Gingercake Rd.

1265

Gingercake Acres Rd.

START

Barkhouse Picnic Area

PNF 496

Mountain-to-Sea Trail

Gingercake Mtn.

PNF 210

Sitting Bear Mtn.

LINVILLE GORGE WILDERNESS

Linville River

Lettered Rock Ridge

Hawksbill Mtn.

PNF 496

PNF 210

Tablerock Mtn.

PNF 210B

Picnic Area

PNF 99

0.0   Ride north on NC 181
0.5   Barkhouse Picnic Area on left.
2.5   Left on paved Gingercake Road.
2.8   Left at fork on paved Gingercake
      Acres Road (1265).
3.8   Enter national forest; begin gravel.
5.4   Sitting Bear Trailhead.
6.4   Hawksbill Trailhead.
7.4   Spence Horse Trail.
8.4   Right at signed junction for Table
      Rock Picnic Area on PNF Road 210B.
10.0 Right on paved PNF Road 99.
11.4 Table Rock Picnic Area; retrace
      route PNF Road 99.
12.9 Left on PNF Road 210B back to
      junction with PNF Road 210.
14.4 Right on PNF Road 210 and
      enter loop.
14.5 Left on PNF Road 496; now New
      Gingercake Road.
22.1 Wilson Creek Trailhead and NC 181.

22. TABLE ROCK

0   0.5   1mi
0   0.5   1km

N

© The Countryman Press

Table Rock

- **DISTANCE:** The ride is a 22.1-mile loop. The Short and Sweet version is a 16.1-mile loop. The Extra Credit ride is a 49-mile loop around Linville Gorge.

- **TERRAIN:** The ride is mostly on gravel and some paved roads in the Grandfather Ranger District of the Pisgah National Forest. It includes a very steep side trip to the Table Rock Trailhead and Picnic Area.

- **SPECIAL FEATURES:** Access to Linville Gorge, and the Table Rock Trailhead.

- **GENERAL LOCATION:** About 12 miles from Linville Falls Visitor Center on the Blue Ridge Parkway.

- **MAPS:** Linville Gorge Wilderness, Pisgah National Forest is available from Pisgah National Forest Offices.

- **ACCESS:** From the junction of NC 181 and NC 183 near Linville Falls on the Blue Ridge Parkway, drive south on NC 181 toward Morganton. In 5.6 miles, reach a trailhead parking area on the left for the Wilson Creek area and the Mountains-to-Sea Trail.

The Table Rock Loop skirts the east edge of Linville Gorge, a rugged and beautiful area that was one of the first areas in the eastern United States designated by Congress as a wilderness area. Though the 10,975-acre wilderness is off-limits to bicycles, the areas surrounding the wilderness are steep and scenic as well. To reach the sheer, better-not-slip overlooks above Linville Gorge,

A rock overhang offers shelter along the hiking trail to Table Rock

you'll have to venture some off the loop, either by taking the side trip to Table Rock Picnic Area and a short walk, or by walking up Hawksbill Trail to another overlook.

A rule you'll quickly learn in exploring the backcountry is that roads always get worse the farther away you get from the highway. But all rules have their exceptions, and Table Rock is the one that proves this rule wrong. For after riding 6 miles of well-worn gravel, this route comes to Pisgah National Forest (PNF) Road 99, a strip of smooth black asphalt, a paved road in the middle of nowhere.

This remarkable road has another characteristic that may explain why, of all the access roads around Linville Gorge Wilderness, it alone was paved. It is probably the steepest road many of us will ever ride. The ride up is a low-gear, slow-motion struggle with gravity, and the white-knuckle descent down hairpin-tight switch-backs can be even more challenging if your brakes are not precisely tuned. You can imagine frustrated forest service engineers struggling for years to keep this near-vertical route in good shape before throwing in the towel and deciding it would be cheaper just to go ahead and pave it. The rewards of the climb up are access to the short trail to the top of Table Rock Mountain and the spectacular views into the 2,000-foot-deep Linville Gorge.

0.0 From the Wilson Creek Trailhead, turn right and ride uphill on NC 181.
The first 2.8 miles of this ride follow North Carolina Bike Route 2. After following the Blue Ridge Parkway for 131 miles, Bike Route 2 leaves the parkway at NC 181 and descends the steep Blue Ridge escarpment before turning east again on NC 90. NC 181 can be busy, but there is a shoulder to ride on.

The Wilson Creek area is less famous than neighboring Linville Gorge but is still a favorite with local hikers.

0.5 Pass Barkhouse Picnic Area on the left.
This alternate parking area usually closes around November for the winter season.

2.5 Turn left on the paved Gingercake Road.

2.8 Turn left at a fork on the paved Gingercake Acres Road (County Road 1265), which may also be signed as TABLE R OCK.
The next mile leads through the Gingercake Development.

3.8 Enter the Pisgah National Forest where the road turns from asphalt to gravel.
You will now enjoy a gentle downhill ride on PNF Road 210, also called Rich Cove Road. The road may be rough, and may have washboards, but at least it is downhill for the next 4.6 miles.

5.4 Pass the Sitting Bear Trailhead on your right.
This is the first of a number of trailheads leading west off PNF Road 210 into Linville Gorge Wilderness.

6.4 Pass the Hawksbill Trailhead and parking area.
If you are not planning to make the steep ride and short hike to the top of Table Rock, the 0.7-mile climb to the top of Hawksbill Mountain is your best opportunity to reach an overlook above Linville Gorge.

7.4 Pass parking areas that mark the start of Spence Horse Trail.

7.8 The Mountains-to-Sea Trail joins the road at a large parking area.
In about 100 yards, the trail will turn left off the road.

8.4 Turn right at a signed junction for Table Rock Picnic Area on PNF Road 210B.
To skip the side trip to Table Rock, continue straight and follow the directions from mile 14.4.

9.1 On the crest of a small hill, pass the entry to North Carolina Outward Bound.

10.0 Turn right on the paved PNF Road 99.
Actually, these directions should say "Take a nice long break and then turn right." The road beyond climbs nearly 900 feet in less than 1.5 miles, at a grade of nearly 12 percent, which is steeper than many hiking trails. You'll need at least a breather before starting this climb. The road may be closed to vehicles during certain times of the year. A sign at the bottom of the road indicates that it is a dead end and has no parking, but in fact, there is ample parking at the trailhead. Gravel PNF Road 99 leading left at this intersection is blocked by a gate.

11.4 Reach Table Rock Picnic Area.
The picnic area has tables, a rest room, and a sign board, which includes a map of Linville Gorge Wilderness. The picnic area also is a trailhead for the Mountains-to Sea Trail and the trail to the top of Table Rock. Table Rock may be closed during the winter season from November until April.

To make the 2-mile, round-trip hike to Table Rock, follow the Mountains-to-Sea Trail to the north into the wilderness area. Trails in the wilderness area are not signed. You will pass less-traveled trails branching right, then left, before leaving the Mountains-to-Sea Trail on a side trail leading right to the summit of Table Rock. After enjoying summit views of Linville Gorge, retrace your route to the parking area and ride very carefully down PNF Road 99.

12.9 Turn left on PNF Road 210B and ride back to the junction with PNF Road 210.

14.4 Turn right on PNF Road 210 and reenter the loop.

14.5 Turn left on PNF Road 496 at a point where the Mountains-to-Sea Trail leaves PNF Road 496.
PNF Road 496 is also called New Gingercake Road. It is closed to motorized use between January 1 and April 1. The road is less traveled, and in better shape, than PNF Road 210. Though several unmaintained gated roads intersect PNF Road 496, there are no major turns between this intersection and NC 181. The bad news is that you will need to climb 400 feet to complete the loop.

14.7 The Mountains-to-Sea Trail turns off the road to the left.

15.4 Pass a gated and unmaintained road on the right.

21.1 The Mountains-to-Sea Trail joins PNF Road 496 from the right.

22.1 Reach the Wilson Creek Trailhead and NC 181.

Short and Sweet: Without the side trip up to the Table Rock Trailhead, the loop is 16.1 miles around.

For Extra Credit: To circle Linville Gorge, connect the gravel Kistler Memorial Highway (NC 1238) near Linville Falls on the west side of the gorge with NC Roads 260, 1254, 1240, 1260, 1258, and finally, 181 to reach the lower end of PNF Road 210. Then ride PNF Road 210 up to NC 181 and return to Linville Falls via NC 181 and NC 183. From the first encounter with NC 181 in the foothills to the second encounter at the Gingercake Development, the route climbs nearly 2,500 feet over a difficult 49 miles.

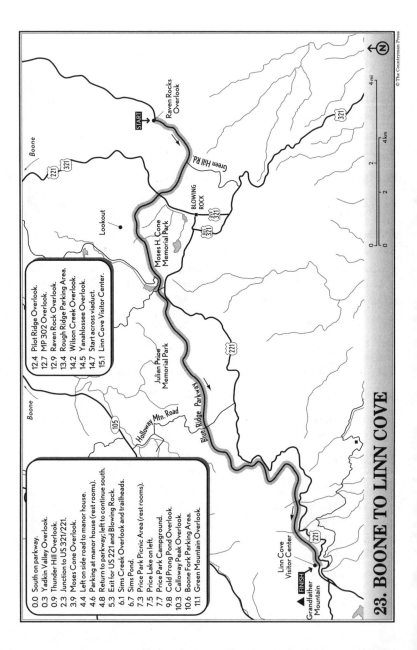

0.0 South on parkway.
0.3 Yadkin Valley Overlook.
0.9 Thunder Hill Overlook.
2.3 Junction to US 321/221.
3.9 Moses Cone Overlook.
4.4 Left on side road to manor house.
4.6 Parking at manor house (rest rooms).
4.8 Return to parkway; left to continue south.
5.3 Exit for US 221 and Blowing Rock.
6.1 Sims Creek Overlook and trailheads.
6.7 Sims Pond.
7.3 Price Park Picnic Area (rest rooms).
7.5 Price Lake on left.
7.7 Price Park Campground.
9.8 Cold Prong Pond Overlook.
10.3 Calloway Peak Overlook.
10.6 Boone Fork Parking Area.
11.1 Green Mountain Overlook.

12.4 Pilot Ridge Overlook.
12.7 MP 302 Overlook.
12.9 Raven Rock Overlook.
13.4 Rough Ridge Parking Area.
14.2 Wilson Creek Overlook.
14.5 Yanahlossee Overlook.
14.7 Start across viaduct.
15.1 Linn Cove Visitor Center.

23. BOONE TO LINN COVE

© The Countryman Press

Boone to Linn Cove

- **DISTANCE:** 15.1 miles one way. The Short and Sweet version is 10.5 miles one way. The Extra Credit ride is 29.8 miles round trip.
- **TERRAIN:** This ride on the Blue Ridge Parkway is difficult and hilly. The longest climb is 1,000 feet to the Linn Cove Viaduct.
- **SPECIAL FEATURES:** The Cone Manor House, views of Grandfather Mountain, and the Linn Cove Viaduct.
- **GENERAL LOCATION:** Outside of Boone and Blowing Rock, North Carolina.
- **MAPS:** Blue Ridge Parkway Official Map and Guide.
- **ACCESS:** From the intersection of the Blue Ridge Parkway and US 321/221 east of Boone and north of Blowing Rock, drive 2.3 miles north on the parkway to Raven Rocks Overlook and park here. Bear in mind there is a similarly named Raven Rocks Overlook near Linn Cove at the end of the ride. To reach the end of the ride from the junction of the parkway and US 221 between Boone and Linville, drive 1.2 miles north on the parkway to Linn Cove Visitor Center.

The Blue Ridge Parkway near the communities of Boone and Blowing Rock is arguably the parkway's most scenic real estate. Cyclists and auto tourists flock to the area to enjoy the splendors of Moses Cone and Julian Price Parks, views of the craggy summits of Grandfather Mountain, and the awesome engineering feat that is the Linn Cove Viaduct. You can combine all these wonders into a single ride if you are willing to ride roads designed by engineers who don't know the meaning of the word flat.

Though you will find traffic heavier here than on other parts of the parkway, you'll also find the road's speed limit has been lowered to 35 mph, perhaps to account for the certainty that most drivers will be sneaking peaks at the scenery. But you'll also have plenty of two-wheeled company, as the riding here is no secret. The Tour DuPont, scene of three straight victories from 1994 to 1996 by a young Lance Armstrong, once passed through these mountains. It was to Boone that Armstrong returned for the epic training sessions that led to his full recovery after he was nearly killed by testicular cancer. Armstrong's turnaround from victim to champion was ignited by a single ride up the course's brutal climb of Beach Mountain. Inspired by memories of his victories and surfing monstrous waves of endorphins, he found again meaning in his life, realizing that "I was meant for a long, hard climb."

Maybe you won't become inspired enough by the riding around Boone to put five consecutive Tour de France victories within your grasp, but surely this is a place to motivate anyone to get on their bike more often and stay on it much longer. In honor of Armstrong's prowess in the mountains, this ride will start at its low point and climb to the Linn Cove Viaduct.

Both Moses Cone and Julian Price Parks are monuments to the generosity of successful businessmen who loved the out-of-doors. Julian Price founded and ran a successful insurance agency. He bought his 4,200-acre estate as a recreation area for company workers. When he died in 1946, the land was donated to the Blue Ridge Parkway.

Moses Cone was a textile mill owner and operator who became famous as the Denim King. Cone and his wife, Bertha, bought their 3,526-acre estate in the 1890s as a place to recover their health and indulge their love of nature. The Cone's built their 23-room home (then called Flat Top Manor), 25 miles of carriage roads, and the Flat Top Mountain Tower. The Cone's philanthropy was widespread. They donated heavily to local schools and helped to found Boone's Appalachian State University. After the death of

Bertha in 1947, the estate passed first to a Greensboro hospital now named for Moses and then to the parkway. The carriage roads remain as the heart of a popular trail network that is closed to bicycles.

The facilities along the Blue Ridge Parkway generally close for the season around the end of October. However, Price Park Picnic Area is open year-round.

0.0 Leave Raven Rocks Overlook (3,834 feet) to travel south on the parkway.

0.3 Pass Yadkin Valley Overlook (3,830 feet) and begin a short climb.

0.9 Pass Thunder Hill Overlook (3,795 feet).
In the distance you can see some of the housing developments surrounding Boone and Blowing Rock.

1.2 Pass Green Hill Road on the left and begin a short descent.

2.3 Reach a junction leading to US 321/221 and resume climbing.

3.9 On the right is overgrown Moses Cone Overlook (3,888 feet).

4.4 Turn left on the side road leading to the Cone Manor House.

4.6 Reach the parking area for the Cone Manor House.
The manor house is the centerpiece of Moses Cone Park. This elegant and well-preserved mansion now houses a visitors center and gift shop operated by the Park Service and Eastern National, the same craft guild that operates the larger shop at the Folk Art Center on the parkway near Asheville, North Carolina. In summer, competition among visitors for the comfy rocking chairs on the front porch is fierce, but the luxury of soaking in the views of Bass Lake and the park's carriage trails makes any wait worthwhile. Should you feel the urge to explore any of the 25 miles of carriage roads, you'll have to walk. Hikers and horseback riders are permitted on the trails, but bicycles are not. Rest rooms are available near the parking area.

4.8 Return to the parkway and turn left to continue your ride to the south.

5.3 Pass an exit for US 221 and Blowing Rock.

6.1 Reach Sims Creek Overlook (3,608 feet) and trailheads for Sims Creek and Green Knob Trails.
The parkway begins to descend.

6.7 Sims Pond (3,447 feet) is on the left.

7.3 Price Park Picnic Area (with rest rooms) is on the right.

7.5 Pass Price Lake on the left.

7.7 The entrance to Price Park Campground is on the right.
Price Park Campground has 129 sites and may be full on popular weekends.

7.9 The boat rental area is on the left.
Begin a gentle climb.

9.3 Pass Hollaway Mountain Road on the right.

The Linn Cove Viaduct protects fragile plant habitats where the Blue Ridge Parkway crosses the slopes of Grandfather Mountain.

9.8 Pass Cold Prong Pond Overlook (3,580 feet).
This curious spot offers no pond and no overlook. Even worse, it marks the start of a steep climb that will ultimately gain over 1,000 feet.

10.3 Pass Calloway Peak Overlook (3,798 feet) on the left where a sign identifies Calloway Peak at 5,964 as the highpoint of the Blue Ridge Mountains.
Calloway Peak is the spectacular highpoint of Grandfather Mountain, but it is by no means the highpoint of the Blue Ridge. The parkway clears 6,000 feet at its highpoint near Richland Balsam, and there are at least 40 other summits in the Southern Appalachians higher than Calloway Peak.

10.6 Pass Boone Fork Parking Area on the right.
This lot can be jammed on summer and fall weekends by hikers heading out on the Tanawha Trail. The Tanawha is a link in the Mountains-to-Sea Trail that connects the Moses Cone and Julian Price Parks with Grandfather Mountain and closely parallels the parkway.

11.1 Pass Green Mountain Overlook (4,134 feet).

12.4 Reach Pilot Ridge Overlook (4,400 feet).
Though there is not much of a view here, this overlook marks the end of the steep climbing.

12.7 Reach Milepost 302 Overlook.
The Wilson Creek drainage is exposed below the parkway, while the rocky expanse of Grandfather Mountain looms above.

12.9 Reach Raven Rocks Overlook (4,400 feet), which offers your initial view of the Linn Cove Viaduct.
This is another trailhead for the Tanawha Trail. The peak you can see in the distance with a tower is Grandmother Mountain.

13.4 Reach Rough Ridge Parking Area (4,291 feet).

14.2 Reach Wilson Creek Overlook.

14.5 Reach Yanahlossee Overlook (4,412 feet).

14.7 Start across the Linn Cove Viaduct.
Tempting as it may be, this is not a safe place to stop for photos.

15.1 Reach Linn Cove Visitor Center.

The Tanawha Trail Trailhead is at the far end of the parking area. The visitors center has interpretive displays, a small bookstore, and rest rooms.

All but 7.5 of the 469 miles of the Blue Ridge Parkway were completed between 1935 and 1967. The final missing link would have to span a rugged and rocky side of Grandfather Mountain and cross delicate and critical plant habitats. Parkway traffic at that time was diverted on US 221, which closely parallels the parkway (you can often see it below). A compromise between environmental concerns and parkway advocates was to build a 1,200-foot-long elevated segment made of interlocking curved masses cast from concrete and supported by seven massive pillars. The viaduct was built between 1979 and 1983 at a cost of almost $10 million. By 1987, the rest of the 7.5-mile missing link, 12 more bridges, and the Tanawha Trail were complete. The now-finished parkway was opened in time for the fall color season of 1987.

Short and Sweet: Start at the Cone Manor House for a 10.5-mile, one-way ride to the Linn Cove Visitor Center.

For Extra Credit: Do this ride as an out-and-back for a total of 29.8 miles (assuming only one visit to the Cone Manor House). Or, extend the ride 1.4 miles south to Beacon Heights Parking Area and trailhead near the junction with US 221 and the entrance to Grandfather Mountain.

24

Flatwoods

- **DISTANCE:** An 18.6-mile loop. The Short and Sweet version is a 6.2-mile loop. The Extra Credit ride is a 28.6-mile loop.

- **TERRAIN:** Though not as level as its name suggests, this loop uses two gently rolling gated forest roads and one lightly traveled, well-maintained gravel road in the Cherokee National Forest. This otherwise easy loop contains 0.5 mile of rocky singletrack.

- **SPECIAL FEATURES:** Plentiful views of Holston Mountain and swimming access for South Holston Lake.

- **GENERAL LOCATION:** About 18 miles east of Bristol, Tennessee and Virginia.

- **MAPS:** Trails Illustrated South Holston and Watauga Lakes, Cherokee National Forest, TN #783.

- **ACCESS:** From the intersection of US 421 and TN 394/435 east of Bristol, drive east on US 421. At 12 miles, turn right on the paved Camp Tom Howard Road (look for signs for Little Oak Campground). The road becomes gravel and is called Cherokee National Forest (CNF) Road 87, or Flatwoods Road, at 12.3 miles. At 12.9 miles, reach a gravel parking area on the left for the signed FLATWOODS HORSE TRAIL.

Flatwoods Horse Trail and Flatwoods Road trace a gentle loop below the rugged crest of Holston Mountain and above the quiet waters of South Holston Lake. The horse trail is a multiple use

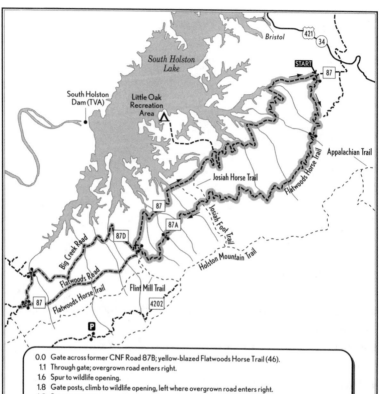

0.0   Gate across former CNF Road 87B; yellow-blazed Flatwoods Horse Trail (46).

1.1   Through gate; overgrown road enters right.

1.6   Spur to wildlife opening.

1.8   Gate posts, climb to wildlife opening, left where overgrown road enters right.

4.3   Stream crossing.

5.2   Four-way junction at end of CNF Road 87B; left on yellow-blazed singletrack, Flatwoods Horse Trail.

5.3   Keep right where trail continues up slope; right again where old road splits left.

5.7   Right at unsigned junction with old road.

5.8   Left at T-junction with CNF Road 87A, gated gravel road.

6.5   Josiah Horse Trail; option.

6.7   Old road enters right.

6.9   Sign for Josiah Hiking Trail.

7.8   Cross gate; begin climbing.

8.5   Spur right to wildlife opening.

9.4   Keep right on CNF Road 87B at signed junction; Flatwoods Horse Trail splits left.

9.7   Right on Flatwoods Road (CNF Road 87) at four-way intersection.

11.6   Wide turnout to swimming area.

11.7   Josiah Hiking Trail (50) begins on right.

12.0   Lower end of Josiah Horse Trail.

13.0   CNF Road 87G leads to Little Oak Recreation Area; straight.

18.6   Flatwoods Horse Trailhead.

24. FLATWOODS

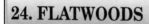

route that includes 0.5 mile of singletrack trail to connect two gated former logging roads (CNF Road 87A and CNF Road 87B). The trail receives light use by horseback riders, and even lighter use by mountain bikers. The gravel surfaces still make for smooth, fast riding, except in midsummer, when they may become a bit clogged by weeds.

The lower slopes of Holston Mountain were once heavily logged, but much of the vast network of old logging roads is gradually disappearing as Mother Nature heals and the forest grows more mature. The ride connects with two hiking trails that climb steeply to the crest of Holston Mountain. The hiking trails are closed to mountain bikers. Unfortunately, these trails have received little maintenance in recent years, and they too are fading into the forest. Riders may encounter hunters along some of the old roads.

The nearby Little Oak Recreation Area has a spacious campground that provides the perfect base camp for exploring the south shore of South Holston Lake.

0.0 The ride begins at the gate across former CNF Road 87B, which is now closed to motorized vehicles.
Flatwoods Horse Trail is CNF Trail 46, and where blazed, is marked in yellow.

1.1 Go through a gate where an overgrown road enters on the right.
In 100 yards, the first of a number of faint spur trails will lead up the mountain.

1.6 A spur road leads left to a wildlife opening.
The Forest Service uses these small openings to improve wildlife habitat. The boundary between trees and meadow is one of the biologically most productive areas in a forest and critical habitat for browsers such as white-tailed deer.

1.8 Just beyond a set of gate posts, climb a dirt bank to reach another wildlife opening.
Turn left at the opening where an overgrown old road enters on the right. The trail beyond follows a gently rolling path along the lower slope of Holston Mountain.

4.3 Cross a small stream and begin a long downhill.

5.2 Reach a four-way junction at the end of CNF Road 87B.

Turn left on a narrow, yellow-blazed singletrack, which is signed FLATWOODS HORSE TRAIL. *The trail may be mislabeled as Trail 56 instead of Trail 46.*

5.3 Keep right where a narrow trail continues up the slope.
Keep right again where another old road splits off left.

5.7 Go right at an unsigned junction with an old road.

5.8 Turn left at a T-junction with CNF Road 87A, which is a gated gravel road very similar in character to CNF Road 87B.
In fact, it seems that you could have used the road to the right to bypass the single-track section, but surprisingly, this road does not connect to CNF Road 87B.

6.5 Reach a signed junction with Josiah Horse Trail (CNF Trail 45), which leads 0.7 mile down to Flatwoods Road (CNF Road 87).
This is a good bail-out option for the main loop or could serve as the end of the Short and Sweet version. If you use Josiah Horse Trail, watch out for a few steep sections where you want to walk your bike, even when heading downhill.

6.7 An old road enters on the right.
This may be the route the Josiah Hiking Trail (CNF Trail 50) uses to climb from Flatwoods Road. However, the trail, like many hiking trails in this part of the CNF, is not signed or blazed.

6.9 At a sign, Josiah Hiking Trail turns left up the mountain.
The number on the post here (also 56) appears to be in error. The CNF inventory lists it as CNF Trail 50.

7.8 Cross a gate and begin climbing.

8.5 A spur road right leads to a wildlife opening.

9.0 Crest a small ridge and begin a welcome descent.

9.4 Keep right on CNF Road 87B at a signed junction where Flatwoods Horse Trail splits off left.
The horse trail follows a two-track dirt road for 0.25 mile and then turns left on a rocky road that receives heavy ATV use. Just beyond the intersection, the horse trail splits off left to follow a rough singletrack, and the riding quickly becomes rocky and difficult. The road with ATV use may be Flint Mill Hiking Trail (CNF Trail 49), which leads 1.4 miles to Flint Mill Gap on the crest of Holston Mountain, but the trail is not marked on this lower end.

South Holston Lake near Flatwoods is popular for boating, fishing, and swimming.

9.7 Turn right on Flatwoods Road (CNF Road 87) at a four-way intersection; there is a gate across CNF Road 87A.
Flatwoods Road also leads left about 5 miles to the west end of Flatwoods Horse Trail. Directly across the intersection is Big Creek Road (CNF Road 87D). These roads can be combined to add ten miles to your loop.

10.4 There is an unofficial camping area with views of Holston Mountain at the head of a gated road on the left.

11.6 A wide turnout marks the start of a path down to an unofficial swimming area on South Holston Lake.

11.7 The blue-blazed Josiah Hiking Trail (CNF Trail 50) begins on the right.
About 50 yards ahead, where gated roads leave either side of the road, is a pullout for parking.

12.0 At a muddy pullout , reach the lower end of Josiah Horse Trail, which leads 0.7 mile up to Flatwoods Horse Trail.

13.0 Go straight where the gravel CNF Road 87G leads 1.85 miles left to Little Oak Recreation Area.
Little Oak offers a 72-site campground, boat access, and short hiking and biking trails, but no designated swimming area. The campground is rarely full. Beyond the campground, expect a few more cars on CNF Road 87 (chances are you've seen few to this point).

14.8 Pass a gated dirt road on the right.

15.7 Pass another gated dirt road on the right.

17.5 There is an unofficial campsite with lake access on the left.

17.7 The bermed road leading left is CNF Road 87H.

18.6 Return to Flatwoods Horse Trailhead.

Short and Sweet: Ride a 6.2-mile loop from the trailhead for Josiah Horse Trail on CNF Road 87. Ride west on CNF Road 87, then join Flatwoods Horse Trail at the junction with CNF Road 87A. Return on Josiah Horse Trail, which starts as an easy singletrack but contains at least two pitches where prudent riders will want to walk their bikes.

For Extra Credit: Flatwoods Horse Trail continues west another 5.4 miles to rejoin CNF Road 87, but 0.25 mile after leaving CNF Road 87B, the trail turns to rough singletrack. For a gentler loop that would also add about 10 miles to your ride, add a loop between Flatwoods Road (CNF Road 87) and Big Creek Road (CNF Road 87D).

25

Doughton to Cumberland

- **DISTANCE:** 23.7 miles one way. The Short and Sweet version is 11.2 miles one way. The Extra Credit ride is 47.4 miles round trip.

- **TERRAIN:** This ride through rolling farms and forests is much gentler than the more mountainous sections of the Blue Ridge Parkway farther south. The longest climb is 300 feet to reach Air Bellows Overlook.

- **SPECIAL FEATURES:** Historic Brinegar Cabin and the scenery at Fox Hunter Paradise.

- **GENERAL LOCATION:** 9 miles south of Galax, Virginia.

- **MAPS:** Blue Ridge Parkway Official Map and Guide.

- **ACCESS:** From the intersection of US 21 and the Blue Ridge Parkway, drive north on the parkway for 12 miles and leave a vehicle at Cumberland Knob Picnic Area at milepost 217.5. From the intersection of US 21 and the parkway, drive south 11.7 miles to Doughton Park. Park in the overflow lots adjacent to the coffee shop and gas station near milepost 241. The north end of the ride is 20 miles south of the intersection of I-77 and the parkway.

The northernmost section of the Blue Ridge Parkway in North Carolina has more in common with a scenic country road than the rugged mountain highways that make up the parkway farther south. Here the scenery is a mix of small farms and patches of forest on rolling hills that is apt to leave you humming a John

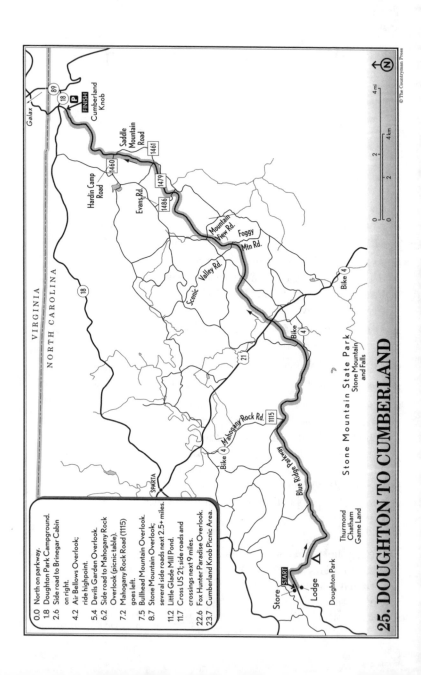

25. DOUGHTON TO CUMBERLAND

0.0   North on parkway.
1.8   Doughton Park Campground.
2.6   Side road to Brinegar Cabin on right.
4.2   Air Bellows Overlook; ride highpoint.
5.4   Devils Garden Overlook.
6.2   Side road to Mahogany Rock Overlook (picnic table).
7.2   Mahogany Rock Road (1115) goes left.
7.5   Bullhead Mountain Overlook.
8.7   Stone Mountain Overlook; several side roads next 2.5+ miles.
11.2 Little Glade Mill Pond.
11.7 Cross US 21; side roads and crossings next 9 miles.
22.6 Fox Hunter Paradise Overlook.
23.7 Cumberland Knob Picnic Area.

VIRGINIA

NORTH CAROLINA

Galax

Cumberland Knob

Saddle Mountain Road

Hardin Camp Road

Evans Rd.

Mountain View Rd.

Foggy Mtn Rd.

Scenic Valley Rd.

Mahogany Rock Rd.

Blue Ridge Parkway

SPARTA

Store

Lodge

Doughton Park

Thurmond Chatham Game Land

Stone Mountain State Park
Stone Mountain and Falls

© The Countryman Press

Denver tune. Also, in contrast to the limited-access parkway sections farther south, this stretch intersects a number of local and county roads. Still, traffic volume is light, and drivers, in general, are accustomed to, and accommodating of, cyclists.

This ride links the two highlights of the parkway in northernmost North Carolina. Doughton Park is a 6,430-acre parcel featuring a lodge (which books nearly full early in the year), campground, picnic area, and 26-mile system of hiking trails. If you're looking to camp anywhere along the parkway, this is the place. The campground has exceptionally large and widely spaced sites. The park was named for 40-year North Carolina congressman "Muley Bob" Doughton, who fought long and hard to build the parkway in his home state.

Though Cumberland Knob will be the end of your ride, it was literally the starting point of the parkway. In the Depression-era of the 1930s, land was especially cheap in this area, so the government was able to make some of its first right-of-way acquisitions for the parkway here. The first stretch of parkway to be built was in 1935 near the picnic area. The current visitors center was the first structure completed by the Civilian Conservation Corps along the parkway. The building now hosts a gift shop, an information station, and rest rooms. Cumberland Knob is a 2,000-acre park and offers a 0.5-mile hike to a shelter atop the knob and a 2-mile hiking trail along Gully Creek.

The facilities at Doughton Park and Cumberland Knob generally close for the winter season at the end of October.

0.0 Turn left on the parkway to begin riding north.

0.2 Pass milepost 241.

0.4 Pass a side road to an overlook on the right.

1.8 Pass Doughton Park Campground on the left.
This spacious and well-maintained campground has 110 sites, all relatively private. In 2003, the fee was $14 per night.

2.6 Pass a short side road to Brinegar Cabin on the right.
This cabin is a reminder of what life was like for pioneer families in the Blue Ridge

before the coming of the parkway. Built in the 1880s, the cabin is a pretty log structure with rough wood siding, glass windows, and two stone-stack chimneys. One storage building, a springhouse, and an outhouse complete the homestead. Inside the cabin is an old loom and weaving exhibit. Outside is a pioneer garden.

The parking area is also the trailhead for Bluff Mountain Trail, which leads 7.5 miles along the parkway to Basin Cove Overlook, and for Cedar Ridge Trail, which leads down 4.4 miles to Grassy Gap Fire Road.

3.9 Pass Road 1130 leading right at Air Bellows Gap.

4.2 Reach Air Bellows Overlook and the highest elevation on the ride at 3,729 feet.

5.4 Reach Devils Garden Overlook.
North Carolina's Mountains-to-Sea Trail has followed the Blue Ridge Parkway for over 300 miles from Great Smoky Mountains National Park to this point. Though the trail is not yet complete, planners expect this overlook will be the point where the parkway and trail part ways. The hiking trail will turn east toward Stone Mountain and lead through the foothills and piedmont to reach the waters of the Atlantic in another 600 miles.

6.2 Reach the short side road to Mahogany Rock Overlook (3,420 feet).
There is a picnic table here if you'd like to linger and enjoy the views. The next part of the ride is downhill and has many more fine vistas.

7.2 Continue straight on the parkway where a gated dirt road leaves right and the paved Mahogany Rock Road (1115) turns left.
Mahogany Rock Road is also North Carolina Bike Route 4, the North Trace Line, which will follow the parkway for the next 3 miles. To the north, Mahogany Rock Road is narrow and has no shoulder. There is limited parking on the shoulder of the road.

7.5 Reach the small Bullhead Mountain Overlook (3,200 feet).

8.7 Reach Stone Mountain Overlook.
Stone Mountain is the centerpiece of a 13,000-acre state park. The shear rock face was formed from an injection of a mass of granite into metamorphic rocks. The granite proved more durable than the rocks around it, which were gradually eroded over time, revealing the 600-foot dome with its distinctive smooth surface. The park preserves a number of historic structures, and along with adjacent state

game lands to the west, provides valuable wildlife habitat. However, recreation is the big drawing card. Not surprisingly, rock climbers are drawn to the high steep cliffs. Fishing and hiking (an 8-mile trail network) are also popular.

9.4 Pass the gravel Polo Road (1110) on the left.

9.8 Pass the gravel Chester Bar Road (1109) on the left and Vestal Road (1109) on the right.

10.3 Pass Rash Road (1108) on the right and Pulltail Road (1111) on the left. *NC Bike Route 4 leaves the parkway on Rash Road, which is narrow and has no shoulder. After a short stretch on Rash Road, Bike Route 4 will turn south on US 21.*

11.2 Reach Little Glade Mill Pond (2,709 feet) at milepost 230. *Beside the Mill Pond is a popular picnic area. There is also a 0.4-mile hiking trail around the pond.*

Brinegar Cabin at Doughton Park along the Blue Ridge Parkway

11.7 Cross US 21, which leads north to Sparta, North Carolina and south to Roaring Gap, North Carolina.

12.1 Pass the paved Pinewood Lane on the right and the gravel Caudill Road (1408) on the left.

14.9 Pass Foggy Mountain Road (1472) on the right.
Just beyond, pass Scenic Valley Road (1433) on the left.

15.8 Cross Mountain View Road (1463).
The road beyond descends to cross Pine Creek on a high bridge and then climbs gently.

18.0 Cross the gravel Evans Road, which is #1479 to the right and #1486 to the left.

19.4 Cross Saddle Mountain Church Road (1461).

20.8 Continue straight at an intersection with Hardin Camp Road (1460) on the left and Saddle Mountain Church Road (1461) on the right.
Enjoy open vistas of rolling valleys on this gentle stretch.

22.6 Reach Fox Hunter Paradise Overlook.
The views across the woods and meadows here are exceptional. Blossoms of rhododendron linger along the roadside into midsummer. There is a 0.2-mile hiking trail to the overlook with views north to Pilot Knob.

23.2 Reach milepost 218.

23.7 Reach Cumberland Knob Picnic Area (2,737 feet).

Short and Sweet: The ride from the coffee shop and gas station at Doughton Park to the Mill Pond is 11.2 miles one way and mostly downhill.

For Extra Credit: If you have only one vehicle and must do this as an out-and-back ride, it is a 47.4-mile round trip. Riding all the way to I-77 will add another 20 miles to your journey.

26

Virginia Creeper

- **DISTANCE:** 18 miles one way from the Whitetop Station Trailhead to Damascus. The Short and Sweet version is 13.3 miles one way. The Extra Credit ride is 69 miles round trip.

- **TERRAIN:** The ride drops 1,600 feet down a converted rail bed through Mount Rogers National Recreation Area and the town of Damascus, Virginia.

- **SPECIAL FEATURES:** Use one of many shuttle services in Damascus to haul you up to Whitetop Station, then you'll follow scenic Laurel Creek downhill back to town.

- **GENERAL LOCATION:** Shuttle services operate out of Damascus, Virginia.

- **MAP:** The brochure, Virginia Creeper National Recreation Trail–Mount Rogers National Recreation Area, is available from the George Washington and Jefferson National Forests.

- **ACCESS:** If you are not using a shuttle, Whitetop Station can be reached by driving east from Damascus on US 58, then turning south on VA Road 726.

The Virginia Creeper National Recreation Trail is a converted railroad line, linking the high heartland of Mount Rogers National Recreation Area with the arts and history-steeped town of Abington, Virginia. The trail is named for the railroad trains that slowly crept from the valley floor to the mountaintop, hauling timber, iron ore, freight, and passengers.

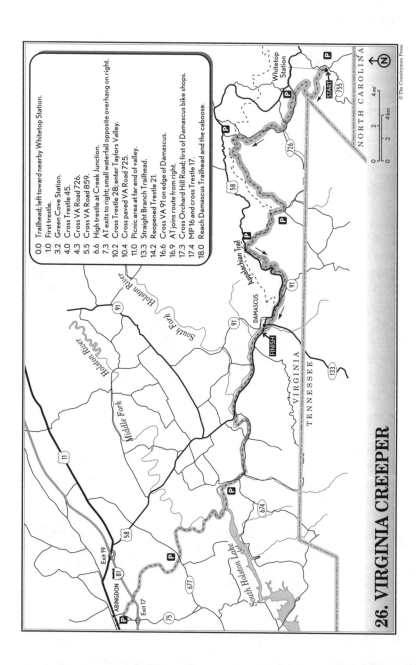

26. VIRGINIA CREEPER

0.0 Trailhead; left toward nearby Whitetop Station.
1.0 First trestle.
3.2 Green Cove Station.
4.0 Cross Trestle 45.
4.3 Cross VA Road 726.
5.5 Cross VA Road 859.
6.6 High trestle at Creek Junction.
7.3 AT exits to right; small waterfall opposite overhang on right.
10.2 Cross Trestle 28; enter Taylors Valley.
10.4 Cross paved VA Road 725.
11.0 Picnic area at far end of valley.
13.3 Straight Branch Trailhead.
14.2 Reopened Trestle 21.
16.6 Cross VA 91 on edge of Damascus.
16.9 AT joins route from right.
17.3 Cross Orchard Hill Road; first of Damascus bike shops.
17.4 MP16 and cross Trestle 17.
18.0 Reach Damascus Trailhead and the caboose.

NORTH CAROLINA

Whitetop Station

START

155

726

58

Appalachian Trail

DAMASCUS

91

91

FINISH

VIRGINIA

TENNESSEE

133

Holston River

South Fork Holston River

Middle Fork

11

Holston River

ABINGDON

Exit 19

81

58

Exit 17

75

677

674

South Holston Lake

N

0   2   4 km
0   2   4 mi

© The Countryman Press

In the early days business was brisk as the railroad brought raw materials down from the mountains and supplies up from the valley. But from the 1930s to the 1970s, the rail line lost money, so the Norfolk and Western Railroad was forced to petition the Interstate Commerce Commission to abandon the line. The company left the railroad unrepaired after a 1977 flood, effectively ending any hope that rail service would be revived. The right-of-way for the eastern portion of the rail line was eventually transferred to the Forest Service, while the western end was transferred to the City of Abington and the Town of Damascus.

Though the Virginia Creeper's route was steep for fully loaded railroad engines, it is not a challenge for most cyclists. The gentle grades, absence of traffic, and nonstop scenery make it perhaps the most popular ride in the region. During mid-season, as many as five bicycle shuttle outfitters operate out of Damascus, Virginia, near the midpoint of the trail. Be sure to make reservations in advance if you plan to use their services.

To ride the Virginia Creeper, most people hire one of the shuttle operators who will ferry riders and bicycles to the Whitetop Station Trailhead for a small fee. The ride back to Damascus is 18 scenic miles of all downhill bliss. The fast pace and wide-open terrain will make you feel ready for the Tour de France. You can easily ride any, or all, of the trail without a shuttle. But if you are new to the sport, not in top biking shape, or just want some easy cruising, this is the ride for you. If you ride on a fair weather weekend, you'll have the company of retired couples, young families, and scout groups, as well as avid cyclists. The Virginia Creeper has become one of the region's outdoor recreation stars. It's a must-ride for any cyclist.

Just because it's easy, don't rush it. You'll miss out on the Virginia Creeper's visual impact. Much of the trail follows scenic Green Cove and Laurel Creeks, repeatedly crossing them on nearly 30 trestles. The longest and highest are sky-high viewing platforms. Most of the trail is in Mount Rogers National Recreation Area, but some of it also passes by scenic mountain farms and small communities, relics from less hectic times.

0.0 Your shuttle operator will drop you off at the busy Whitetop Station Trailhead.

From the parking area, turn left and ride toward nearby Whitetop Station. To the right the trail extends another 1 mile to the North Carolina state line, beyond which there is no longer public access to the rail bed. Whitetop Station has flush toilets and a small museum, perfect for an introduction to the area's rich history.

0.8 Pass milepost 33.

The large concrete monuments left over from the original rail line help you tick off the miles. Smaller metal mileposts, which help to point out other special features, were installed after the rail line was converted to trail. There's enough grade on these upper reaches that rolling all the way to Damascus seems possible.

1.0 Reach the trail's first trestle.

The trail's many trestles are another highlight of the ride. They range from short bridges over small creeks to long elevated spans above Laurel Creek.

2.8 The trail crosses a small gravel road.

3.2 Arrive at Green Cove Station.

Green Cove Station and Trailhead are accessible from US 58 on the paved VA Road 600. The visitors center here is operated seasonally and features a small museum and pit toilets. Here the trail joins Green Cove Creek, which it will follow to its confluence with Laurel Creek.

4.0 Cross Trestle 45 near one of the many Christmas tree farms that flourish on the private lands within the borders of Mount Rogers National Recreation Area.

4.3 Cross VA Road 726.

5.5 Cross VA Road 859.

The trail now enters the woods with frequent views of Green Cove Creek. To this point, the Virginia Creeper has been a thin ribbon of public land winding through inholdings of Mount Rogers National Recreation Area. With the exception of a short trip through Taylors Valley, most of your remaining ride to the outskirts of Damascus is across public land.

6.6 The long high trestles at Creek Junction are the most impressive of all the bridges along the Virginia Creeper.

Riders at Whitetop Station

Here Green Cove Creek flows into Laurel Creek, which the trail will follow to Damascus. The Appalachian Trail also briefly joins the Virginia Creeper at Trestle 38. If really long trips are your thing, drop your bike, turn right on the Appalachian Trail, and follow the white blazes for almost 1,700 miles to the trail's end on Mount Katahdin in Maine.

7.1 Road 728 leads to a stream access point and the Creek Junction Trailhead.

7.3 The Appalachian Trail exits to the right, just before reaching another large trestle.
The trails will merge one more time before reaching Damascus together. Just beyond the split, look for a small waterfall opposite a rock overhang on the right side of the trail. This shady dell is perfect for a midride rest stop.

10.2 After crossing Trestle 28, enter Taylors Valley.
If you're running low on supplies, there is a small store and cafe in the valley just south of the trail. Remember to be especially careful and courteous riding through this area because the narrow trail corridor is bordered by private property.

10.4 Cross the paved VA Road 725.

11.0 Reach a picnic area at the far end of the valley.
From Taylors Valley the trail enters another beautiful streamside section through the woods along Laurel Creek.

11.3 The Appalachian Trail joins the Virginia Creeper on the right.

13.3 Pass the popular Straight Branch Trailhead, which is just off US 58.
This is a popular starting point for self-sufficient parties who plan to ride to Whitetop Station and back. The Appalachian Trail leaves the Virginia Creeper here.

14.2 Trestle 21 was destroyed in a flash flood on July 29, 2001.
According to Forest Service sources, the entire 120-foot span was simply washed away after flood debris became pinned to the supports of the trestle. Due to cooperative efforts between the Forest Service, the bridge contractor, and trail users, the bridge was replaced and the trail reopened by spring of 2002.
   Trestle 18, just below US 58, is of similar construction.

16.6 Cross VA 91 on the edge of Damascus.
The Virginia Creeper will shadow US 58 through Damascus.

16.9 The Appalachian Trail joins the route from the right.

17.3 Cross Orchard Hill Road next to the first of the bike shops in Damascus.

17.4 Reach milepost 16 and soon cross Trestle 17.

18.0 Reach the Damascus Trailhead by a large parking area and retired caboose that serves as a visitors center and gift shop.
Alvarado is 7 miles farther down the trail, while the end of the trail in Abington is 15.5 miles away. Summer riders should be aware that the trail beyond Damascus is far less shady.

Short and Sweet: This ride is easy enough that almost anyone will be able to ride the full distance back to Damascus. However, if you would like to make the ride just a bit shorter, you can stop at the trailhead along US 58 after just 13.3 miles.

For Extra Credit: A round-trip ride from Abington to the North Carolina state line and back is 69 miles. Many shuttle services will offer to pick you up in Abington and drop you off at Whitetop Station for a 33.5-mile, one-way ride.

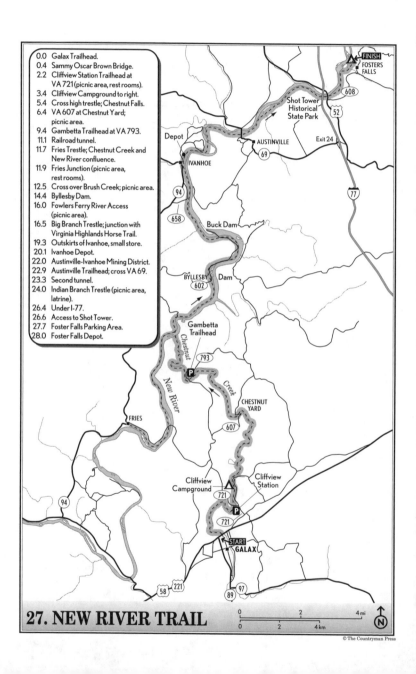

0.0 Galax Trailhead.
0.4 Sammy Oscar Brown Bridge.
2.2 Cliffview Station Trailhead at VA 721 (picnic area, rest rooms).
3.4 Cliffview Campground to right.
5.4 Cross high trestle; Chestnut Falls.
6.4 VA 607 at Chestnut Yard; picnic area.
9.4 Gambetta Trailhead at VA 793.
11.1 Railroad tunnel.
11.7 Fries Trestle; Chestnut Creek and New River confluence.
11.9 Fries Junction (picnic area, rest rooms).
12.5 Cross over Brush Creek; picnic area.
14.4 Byllesby Dam.
16.0 Fowlers Ferry River Access (picnic area).
16.5 Big Branch Trestle; junction with Virginia Highlands Horse Trail.
19.3 Outskirts of Ivanhoe, small store.
20.1 Ivanhoe Depot.
22.0 Austinville-Ivanhoe Mining District.
22.9 Austinville Trailhead; cross VA 69.
23.3 Second tunnel.
24.0 Indian Branch Trestle (picnic area, latrine).
26.4 Under I-77.
26.6 Access to Shot Tower.
27.7 Foster Falls Parking Area.
28.0 Foster Falls Depot.

FINISH
FOSTERS FALLS
608
Shot Tower Historical State Park
52
AUSTINVILLE
69
Exit 24
Depot
IVANHOE
77
94
Buck Dam
658
BYLLESBY Dam
602
Gambetta Trailhead
Chestnut Creek
793
CHESTNUT YARD
607
New River
FRIES
94
Cliffview Campground
Cliffview Station
721
721
START
GALAX
58 221
89 97

27. NEW RIVER TRAIL

0   2   4 mi
0   2   4 km

N

© The Countryman Press

New River Trail

- **DISTANCE:** 28 miles one way from Galax to Foster Falls. The Short and Sweet version is 17.4 miles one way from Galax to Fries. The Extra Credit ride is the entire 49.7-mile trail from Galax to Pulaski.

- **TERRAIN:** A gentle ride along an abandoned rail corridor through New River Trail State Park that drops 350 feet.

- **SPECIAL FEATURES:** An easy ride along scenic Chestnut Creek and the New River.

- **GENERAL LOCATION:** Galax, Virginia, to Foster Falls, Virginia, near the intersection of I-77 and I-81.

- **MAP:** The New River Trail State Park Guide is available from rhe Virginia Department of Conservation and Recreation.

- **ACCESS:** The ride starts in the middle of Galax on US 58, just 0.1 mile north of the junction with VA 89 and across from the massive Vaughn Furniture Plant. To reach Foster Falls from I-77, take Exit 24 and drive east on VA 69 for 0.3 mile to US 52. Follow US 52 north 1.7 miles, then turn east on VA 608, which is Foster Falls Road. In 1.8 miles, turn left on VA 623, which leads to the village of Foster Falls.

New River Trail State Park is a shining example of the value of keeping abandoned rail lines in public hands. The trail is one of the most popular recreation areas in southwest Virginia. It draws both the residents of surrounding towns, who use it regularly for exercise and an escape route to the outdoors, and out-of-towners, who flock to stunning scenery, easy access, and gentle grades of one of the longest rail trails in the Southeast. The trail also has been good for the local economy. Several businesses, including bike shops and shuttle services, have sprung up to support trail users. The easy access and beautiful scenery have made the New River a worth-the-drive-destination for both families and serious cyclists.

The New River Trail cuts a wide swath through the natural and human history of southwest Virginia. The first 12 miles of this route lie along pretty Chestnut Creek, a lively frolicking stream. After joining the New River, the trail passes two dams and enters the historic mining towns of Austinville and Ivanhoe. Finally, the trail passes Shot Tower Historic State Park before reaching Foster Falls.

The New River Trail began its life as the route of the Norfolk and Western Railroad, which was built to service the lead and iron mines that flourished in the region in the late 1800s and early 1900s. When the mines began to shut down, the railroad was also forced to close. The railway serviced towns from Pulaski to Galax between 1904 and 1985. In 1986, Norfolk Southern Corporation donated the abandoned right-of-way to the Virginia Division of State Parks. The state park opened in May 1987 with an initial 4 miles of trail.

New River Trail is the longest and skinniest state park around. The 57-mile trail covers only 765 acres along a corridor only 80 feet wide. Much of the corridor is through private land, so users should respect the surrounding property by staying on the trail. The trail surface is well-maintained packed cinders, which make for smooth, fast riding. The trail is patrolled by rangers in season. Two state park campgrounds at Cliffview and Foster Falls are perfect for bikepackers. Cliffview Campground is accessible only by trail. Both require advance reservations.

The New River Trail has become popular enough to support several shuttle services. It is well worth the small fee to avoid the time and hassle of shuttling cars on your own.

0.0 Start your ride at the Galax Trailhead.
You will ride on an embankment above Chestnut Creek for the next 11 miles. The first few miles pass through farms and scattered home sites.

0.4 Reach Sammy Oscar Brown Bridge.
There is a parking area on a paved road at the far end of the bridge.

0.6 Reach milepost 51, the first of many that will mark your progress toward Foster Falls.
You will also pass some newer metal mileposts along the trail that will not always agree with the mileages on the older and larger mileposts.

2.2 Reach the Cliffview Station Trailhead at VA 721, the road that connects Galax to Fries.
There is parking, a picnic area, a water fountain, rest rooms, a gift shop, and trail information here. The trailhead is also the closest access for the bike-in only Cliffview Campground.

3.4 Pass Cliffview Campground to the right of the trail.
There is no vehicle access to this campground. There are 13 well-spaced sites that must be reserved in advance by calling the state park.

5.4 Cross a high trestle next to Chestnut Falls.
The trail now lies in thick forest.

6.4 Reach VA 607 at Chestnut Yard where there is parking and a picnic area.

9.4 Reach the Gambetta Trailhead at VA 793.
Facilities at Gambetta include parking and a shaded picnic area.

11.1 Reach the first of two railroad tunnels along the trail.
The tunnel is 193 feet long and has enough curve so that the far end is not visible from the entrance. However, it is not so long that a light is needed, and wood braces inside add a feeling of security to the short passage.

11.7 Reach milepost 40 at the 1,089-foot-long Fries Trestle and the conflu-ence of Chestnut Creek and the New River.
In contrast to the rollicking Chestnut Creek, the New River is a quiet backwater, impounded by two dams, which you will pass in the next 6 miles.

11.9 Reach Fries Junction.
This is the only important junction along the entire trail. To the left, Fries Branch

On the Big Branch Trestle along the New River Trail

leads 5.5 miles gently uphill to terminate at the Fries Trailhead. To the right, the trail leads to Foster Falls and eventually to the lower end at Pulaski. There is a picnic area with map board and rest rooms at the junction.

12.5 Cross a trestle over Brush Creek beside another picnic area.

14.4 Pass Billesby Dam and access to VA Road 602.
The dam was completed in 1913 and is operated by the Appalachian Power Company. The trail now runs alongside VA 737, out of sight of the river.

15.6 Cross the gravel Road 737.

16.0 Reach Fowlers Ferry River Access and Picnic Area.
On the riverbank is Ruth's Spring, which may be reduced to a trickle by late summer. Here's another shady spot to rest and watch the river flow.

16.5 Reach Big Branch Trestle and the junction with Virginia Highlands Horse Trail.
A sign indicates that the horse trail leads 5 miles to VA 94, 10 miles to Raven Cliff Horse Camp, and 83 miles to Elk Garden in the heart of the high country of Mount Rogers National Recreation Area.

17.1 Road 737 terminates at Buck Dam.
There is a parking area at the dam, and a picnic area and latrine a bit farther down the trail.

18.7 Cross the gravel Road 658 at milepost 33 by a cluster of homes.

19.3 Pass through the outskirts of Ivanhoe, which has a small store.

20.1 Reach Ivanhoe Depot on VA 639 at the end of a 607-foot-long trestle.
The depot has parking, a picnic area, a rest room, and a map board, as well as a large rock crusher in the corner of the lot.

22.0 Enter the grounds of the old Austinville-Ivanhoe Mining District.
The Austinville Ivanhoe Mining District was one of the most important metal mining areas in the eastern United States. From 1756 to 1981, zinc and lead ores were mined from pits and shafts spread over a 6-mile-long area. By the time the workings were allowed to flood, Austinville had produced 30 million tons of ore, including much of the lead used for ammunition in the Civil War. It was the longest continuously mined base metal deposit in North America. Only a few dilapidated buildings, small rock piles, and pieces of discarded equipment remain from a limestone quarry that succeeded the metal mines.

22.9 Reach the Austinville Trailhead and cross VA 69.
Look for the entrance of a small mine tunnel to the right of the trail.

23.3 Reach the trail's second tunnel.
This one is a bit shorter (135 feet) and straighter.

24.0 Reach Indian Branch Trestle and a picnic area with a latrine.
The trail beyond is tucked between the river and scenic limestone cliffs.

26.4 Cross underneath I-77.

26.6 Reach the access trail to the Shot Tower.
The tower was an innovative solution to the problem of making round shot for muskets and shotguns from the lead ores mined locally. By driving a tunnel from the

river to the bottom of a 75-foot shaft, and then building a 75-foot-high tower above the shaft, the builders created a 150-foot drop. Molten lead was slowly poured down the shaft into pails of water. The long drop shaped the shot, and the water solidified it. The site is now a state historic park.

27.7 Reach Foster Falls Parking Area.

27.8 Pass milepost 24.

28.0 Reach Foster Falls Depot.
The depot has a trail store and information area. A 21-site campground is located next to the New River. There are also rest rooms and telephones at the depot. Foster Falls Village offers a horse livery, boat launch, and bike shop.

Short and Sweet: The ride from Galax to Fries is a beautiful 17.4 miles one way.

For Extra Credit: The entire trail from Galax to Pulaski is 49.7 miles one way. A slightly shorter option would be to ride the 43.3 miles from Fries to Pulaski.

APPENDIX: CONTACT INFORMATION

NATIONAL PARK SERVICE

Blue Ridge Parkway
199 Hemphill Knob Road
Asheville, NC 28801-8636
828-271-4779
www.nps.gov/blri

Chickamauga & Chattanooga National Military Park
P.O. Box 2128
Fort Oglethorpe, GA 30742
706-866-9241
www.nps.gov/chch

Great Smoky Mountains National Park
107 Park Headquarters Road
Gatlinburg, TN 37738
865-436-1200
www.nps.gov/grsm

UNITED STATES FOREST SERVICE

Cherokee National Forest (CNF) Offices
Supervisor's Office
2800 North Ocoee Street

P.O. Box 2010
Cleveland, TN 37320
423-476-9700
www.southernregion.fs.fed.us/cherokee

Watauga Ranger District (CNF)
P.O. Box 400
Unicoi, TN 37692
423-735-1500

Nolichucky-Unaka Ranger Station (CNF)
4900 Asheville Highway SR70
Greenville, TN 37743
423-638-4109

Tellico-Hiwassee Ranger District (CNF)
250 Ranger Station Road
Tellico Plains, TN 37385
423-253-2520

Ocoee-Hiwassee Ranger District (CNF)
3171 Highway 64
Benton, TN 37307
423-338-5201

Ocoee Whitewater Center (CNF)
Route I, Box 285
Highway 64 West
Copperhill, TN 37317
423-496-5197 or
877-692-6050

National Forests in North Carolina (Pisgah PNF and Nantahala NNF)
Supervisor's Office
160A Zillicoa Street
Asheville, NC 28801
828-257-4200
www.cs.unca.edu/nfsnc

Appalachian Ranger District (PNF)
French Broad Station
P.O. Box 128
Hot Springs, NC 28743
828-622-3202

Grandfather Ranger District (PNF)
Route 1, Box 110-A
Nebo, NC 28761
828-652-2144

Appalachian Ranger District (PNF)
Toecane Ranger Station
P.O. Box 128
Burnsville, NC 28714
828-682-6146

Pisgah Ranger District (PNF)
1001 Pisgah Highway
Pisgah Forest, NC 28768
828-877-3265

Cheoah Ranger District (NNF)
Route 1, Box 16A
Robbinsville, NC 28771
828-479-6431

Highlands Ranger District (NNF)
2010 Flat Mountain Road
Highlands, NC 28741
828-526-3765

Tusquitee Ranger District (NNF)
123 Woodland Drive
Murphy, NC 28906
828-837-5152

Wayah Ranger District (NNF)
90 Sloan Road
Franklin, NC 28734
828-524-6441

George Washington and Jefferson National Forests (GWJNF)
Supervisor's Office
5162 Valleypointe Parkway
Roanoke, VA 24019-3050
888-265-0019 or 540-265-5100
www.southernregion.fs.fed.us/gwj

Blacksburg-Wythe Ranger Districts (GWJNF)
155 Sherwood Road
Wytheville, VA 24382
540-228-5551

Mount Rogers National Recreation Area (GWJNF)
3714 Highway 16
Marion, VA 24354-4097
276-783-5196

STATE AND LOCAL TRANSPORTATION DEPARTMENTS AND BICYCLE COORDINATORS

North Carolina Department of Transportation
Division of Bicycle and Pedestrian Transportation
P.O. Box 25201
1 S. Wilmington Street
Raleigh, NC 27602
(or) 1552 Mail Service Center
Raleigh, NC 27699-1552
919-733-2804
www.ncdot.org/transit/bicycle/

Tennessee Department of Transportation
Suite 700, James K. Polk Building
Nashville, TN 37243-0349
www.tdot.state.tn.us/bikeroutes/routes

Virginia Department of Transportation
Virginia State Bicycle Coordinator
1401 East Broad Street
Richmond, VA, 23219
800-835-1203 and 804-371-4869
www.virginiadot.org

City of Asheville
Transportation Services
P.O. Box 7148
Asheville, NC 28802
828-259-5617

Maryville Parks and Recreation
316 South Everett High Road
Maryville, TN 37804
865-981-3302
www.ci.maryville.tn.us

City of Alcoa
223 Associates Boulevard
Alcoa, TN 37701
www.ci.alcoa.tn.us

Maryville, Alcoa, Blount County Parks and Recreation Commission
P.O. Box 789
Alcoa, TN 37701
865-983-9244
www.parksrec.com

Knox County Parks and Recreation
Room 583 City County Building
400 Main Street
Knoxville, TN 37902
865-215-6600
www.rnd.knoxcounty.org/parks/index.html

STATE PARKS AND FORESTS

North Carolina Department of Environment and Natural Resources
Division of Parks and Recreation
1615 MSC
Raleigh, NC 27699
919-733-4181
www.ils.unc.edu/park/project/ncparks.html

Mount Mitchell State Park
2388 State Highway 128
Burnsville, NC 28714
828-675-4611
mount.mitchell@ncmail.net

Stone Mountain State Park
3042 Frank Parkway
Roaring Gap, NC 28668
336-957-8185
stonemtn@infoave.net

House Mountain State Natural Area
(Managed by Knox County)
9601 Hogskin Road
Knoxville, TN 37902

Prentice Cooper State Forest and Wildlife Management Area
P.O. Box 160
Hixson, TN 37343
423-634-3091 or 423-658-5551
www.state.tn.us/agriculture/forestry/stateforests/7.html

Virginia Department of Conservation and Recreation
203 Governor Street, Suite 213
Richmond, VA 23219-2094
804-786-1712
www.dcr.state.va.us/parks

New River Trail State Park
176 Orphanage Drive
Foster Falls, VA 24360
276-699-6778
276-236-8889 (Cliffview office)
800-933-7275 (Campground reservations)
www.dcr.state.va.us/parks/newriver.htm

Grayson Highlands State Park
829 Grayson Highland Lane
Mouth of Wilson, VA 24363
276-579-7092
www.dcr.state.va.us/parks/graysonh.htm

OTHER CYCLING RESOURCES

Blue Blaze Bike and Shuttle Service
(Shuttle Service for Virginia Creeper)
226 West Laurel Avenue
Damascus, VA 24236
800-475-5095 or 276-475-5095
www.blueblazebikeandshuttle.com

The Bike Station
(Shuttle service for Virginia Creeper)
501 E. 3rd Street
Damascus, VA 24236
866-475-3629
www.thebike-station.com

Blue Ridge Bicycle Club, Inc.
P.O. Box 309
Asheville, NC 28802
www.blueridgebicycleclub.org

Chattanooga Bicycle Club
P.O. Box 11495
Chattanooga, TN 37401
www.chattbike.com

Cherry Creek Cyclery & More
116 Orphanage Drive
Foster Falls, VA 24360
276-699-2385 or 1-800-636-4013
www.cccyclery.com

Cradle of Forestry in America Interpretive Association
(Serves national forests in North Carolina)
100 South Broad Street
Brevard, NC 28712
1-800-660-0671 or 828-884-5713
www.cradleofforestry.com

East Tennessee Mountain Bike
(Best Web site for information on mountain biking in Tennessee)
www.cs.utk.edu/~dunigan/mtnbike

Foothills Land Conservancy
614 Sevierville Road
Maryville, TN 37804
865-681-8326
www.foothillsland.org

Mountain Bike Western North Carolina
(An on-line resource for mountain biking in Western North Carolina)
www.mtbikewnc.com

New River Adventures
(Shuttle service for New River Trail)
Foster Falls Village, VA 24360
276-699-1034
www.newriveradventures.com

New River Riders Bike Shoppe
(Shuttle service for New River Trail)
208 East Stuart Drive
Galax, VA 24333
877-510-2572 and 276-236-5900
www.newriverriders.com

Smoky Mountain Convention and Visitors Bureau
7906 East Lamar Alexander Parkway
Townsend, TN 37882-4033
800-525-6384
www.smokymountains.org

Smoky Mountain Wheelmen
P.O. Box 31497
Knoxville, TN 37930
www.smwbike.org

Tennessee Wildlife Resources Foundation
P.O. Box 110031
Nashville, TN 37222
615-831-3480
www.state.tn.us/twra/foundmap.html

Let Backcountry Guides Take You There

Our experienced backcountry authors will lead you to the finest trails, parks, and back roads in the following areas:

50 Hikes Series
50 Hikes in the Adirondacks
50 Hikes in Colorado
50 Hikes in Connecticut
50 Hikes in Central Florida
50 Hikes in North Florida
50 Hikes in South Florida
50 Hikes in the Lower Hudson Valley
50 Hikes in Kentucky
50 Hikes in the Maine Mountains
50 Hikes in Coastal and Southern Maine
50 Hikes in Louisiana
50 Hikes in Massachusetts
50 Hikes in Maryland
50 Hikes in Michigan
50 Hikes in the White Mountains
50 More Hikes in New Hampshire
50 Hikes in New Jersey
50 Hikes in Central New York
50 Hikes in Western New York
50 Hikes in the Mountains of North Carolina
50 Hikes in Ohio
50 More Hikes in Ohio
50 Hikes in Eastern Pennsylvania
50 Hikes in Central Pennsylvania
50 Hikes in Western Pennsylvania
50 Hikes in the Tennessee Mountains
50 Hikes in Vermont
50 Hikes in Northern Virginia
50 Hikes in Southern Virginia
50 Hikes in Wisconsin

Walking
Walks and Rambles on Cape Cod and the Islands
Walks and Rambles on the Delmarva Peninsula
Walks and Rambles in the Western
  Hudson Valley
Walks and Rambles on Long Island
Walks and Rambles in Ohio's Western Reserve
Walks and Rambles in Rhode Island
Walks and Rambles in and around St. Louis
Weekend Walks in St. Louis and Beyond
Weekend Walks Along the New England Coast
Weekend Walks in Historic New England
Weekend Walks in the Historic Washington D.C.
  Region

Bicycling
25 Bicycle Tours in the Adirondacks
25 Bicycle Tours on Delmarva
25 Bicycle Tours in Savannah and the Carolina
  Low Country
25 Bicycle Tours in Maine
25 Bicycle Tours in Maryland
25 Bicycle Tours in the Twin Cities and
  Southeastern Minnesota
30 Bicycle Tours in New Jersey
25 Bicycle Tours in the Hudson Valley
25 Bicycle Tours in the Lake Champlain Region
25 Bicycle Tours in Maryland
25 Bicycle Tours in Ohio's Western Reserve
25 Bicycle Tours in the Texas Hill Country and
  West Texas
25 Bicycle Tours in Vermont
25 Bicycle Tours in and around Washington, D.C.
25 Mountain Bike Tours in the Adirondacks
25 Mountain Bike Tours in the Hudson Valley
25 Mountain Bike Tours in Massachusetts
25 Mountain Bike Tours in New Jersey
Backroad Bicycling in the Blue Ridge and Smoky
  Mountains
Backroad Bicycling in Connecticut
Backroad Bicycling on Cape Cod, Martha's
  Vineyard, and Nantucket
Backroad Bicycling in the Finger Lakes Region
Backroad Bicycling in Western Massachusetts
Backroad Bicycling in New Hampshire
Backroad Bicycling in Eastern Pennsylvania
Backroad Bicycling in Wisconsin
The Mountain Biker's Guide to Ski Resorts
Bicycling America's National Parks: Arizona &
  New Mexico
Bicycling America's National Parks: California
Bicycling America's National Parks: Oregon &
  Washington
Bicycling America's National Parks: Utah &
  Colorado
Bicycling Cuba

We offer many more books on hiking, fly-fishing, travel, nature, and other subjects. Our books are available at bookstores and outdoor stores everywhere. For more information or a free catalog, please call 1-800-245-4151 or write to us at The Countryman Press, P.O. Box 748, Woodstock, Vermont 05091. You can find us on the Internet at www.countryman-press.com.